D0235602

Know Your Rights

A Guide to Everyday Law

Ronald Irving and Charles Anthony

DAVID & CHARLES
Newton Abbot London North Pomfret (VT) Vancouver

ISBN 0 7153 7143 6

Library of Congress Catalog Card Number 76-8664

Reprinted 1976

Set in 10 on 12pt Imprint
and printed in Great Britain
by Biddles Limited, Guildford, Surrey
for David & Charles (Publishers) Limited
Brunel House Newton Abbot Devon

Published in the United States of America
by David & Charles Inc
North Pomfret Vermont 05053 USA

Published in Canada
by Douglas David & Charles Limited
1875 Welch Street North Vancouver BC

Contents

This book is intended as a general guide to everyday law. It should be borne in mind that a reader who has a particular legal problem should consult a solicitor, and that the law is constantly changing – although the chapter on employment law has tried to anticipate certain changes.

This volume deals only with the law of England and Wales. No attempt has been made to cover the laws of Scotland or Northern Ireland.

1 Going to Court

The English Legal System

Our legal system, like the rest of our constitution, is the fruit of experience, not of logic; it is the product of an evolution which began before the Norman Conquest. In its growth, it has drawn from many different sources. It has been shaped by the pressures and accidents of history. In general, political ideologies have only modified it and legal theories only ratified it. It is known as a common law system, and countries which have adopted our system are known as 'common law countries'. Most European countries are 'civil law countries', basing their law on a code derived from Roman law.

The Sources of Law

Case Law

An important factor in case law is the doctrine of precedent. This is the practice whereby lower courts adopt and apply the principles of law set out in decisions of higher courts. The procedure depends upon:

1 An established hierarchy or pyramid of courts

2 An adequate system of reporting cases

The hierarchy of the courts is set out on pp 6–9.

Our system of law depends heavily on the doctrine of precedent and it is the means whereby legal doctrines can be expanded or modified. In reaching a decision any court will make a finding of facts and then apply the relevant principles of law to those facts. It is the application of these principles of law which constitutes the reason (or 'ratio') of the judgement. For example, a judge may find in a case that a car collided with a four-year-old child who unexpectedly ran out of a school playground. The ratio of the case may be that a driver owes a higher duty of vigilance in the proximity of young children who cannot be expected to comprehend the dangers of traffic. The case may then be reported and that ratio will be applied to lower courts when similar problems occur. The particular facts are not relevant.

Lower courts must follow the decisions of higher courts, but courts are not bound by the decisions of equal or inferior courts. Sometimes a case can be 'distinguished' and therefore need not be followed; this is really another way of saying that although at first sight it appears relevant, there are reasons why the principle it established does not apply.

The House of Lords is the highest court in the country. Although it will not lightly override its own past decision, it is free to do so (in restating or interpreting the law). The system of precedent is an attempt to achieve stability without rigidity.

Custom

Even today, time-honoured local customs can have the force of law, as can the established usages of particular trades. However, custom and usage are a relatively minor source of law.

Legislation

Parliament is the supreme law-making authority. It can change even the most well-established rule of law. The courts have no authority to question an Act of Parliament. It is their task, though, to interpret statutes.

With the enormous increase in recent years of social legislation, statute law has become of greater importance in almost every sphere of law. This does not mean that the role of the courts has become any less important. For example, although taxation law is initiated entirely by statute, these statutes then have to be interpreted in the light of innumerable court decisions on their meaning and application.

The Structure of the Courts

The courts are arranged in a pyramid. At the bottom are the magistrates' courts and the county courts, which have entirely separate functions according to the case—civil or criminal. Above them are crown courts, which hear only criminal cases, and the High Court which is mainly civil. Next comes the Court of Appeal, which is both civil and criminal. At the apex of the pyramid is the House of Lords, which is the final court of appeal. However, most cases begin and end in the magistrates' court or the county court.

Magistrates' Courts

1 *Criminal Jurisdiction.* Magistrates' courts are usually presided over by at least two justices of the peace. They are not lawyers but lay men and women appointed by the Lord Chancellor. JPs act in their spare time and are unpaid. To advise them on the law, they will have a clerk, who will usually be a solicitor.

In the larger towns, there are sometimes 'stipendiary' magistrates. These are full-time professionals. They are appointed from solicitors or barristers of some years' standing. Stipendiary magistrates sit alone.

Magistrates' courts try all minor charges, including most motoring offences, assaults, thefts and minor 'revenue' offences, like failure to buy National Insurance stamps or television licences. Some magistrates also preside over juvenile courts, which sit in private and have less formal procedure (see also Chapter 4).

Some offences such as theft and more serious assaults carry the right of trial in the Crown Court at the defendant's choice. The defendant must be told of this right by the clerk to the magistrates' court before he answers the charge. Some other offences can be tried at the Crown Court only if the prosecution so chooses. Certain offences (such as burglary of a dwelling house) can be tried only by the Crown Court. The defendant must then appear before the magistrates who, if satisfied that there is a case against him, will commit him to the Crown Court to stand trial before a judge and jury.

2 *Civil Jurisdiction.* Magistrates' courts also deal with disputes between husband and wife, the custody of children, maintenance and affiliation orders and similar matters.

Magistrates' courts cannot grant divorces but they can make separation orders. However, now that divorce can be obtained on the grounds of breakdown of marriage, separation orders are becoming less common.

Nonetheless, the magistrates' courts are still very important as they provide help quickly and cheaply for people with domestic problems. For instance, if a husband is neglecting to provide for his wife or is guilty of persistent cruelty, she may apply for an order against him. Apart from being immediately useful, the order may be used as evidence in later divorce proceedings. A magistrate's order giving custody of the children may likewise be useful in settling the immediate dispute over custody.

County Courts

Civil Jurisdiction Only. County courts have a misleading name because the areas which they serve bear no relation to the administrative counties but are much smaller. They hear most civil cases. There are in fact over 350 county courts. The relevant court for any case will be the one in whose area the defendant lives or carries on business or the one in whose area the action complained of occurred.

Cases in a county court will be heard by a single 'circuit judge'. Again, he will have been a solicitor or barrister and have been appointed by the Lord Chancellor. (Lesser cases can be heard by a registrar.) In the county court, the judge will deal only with civil cases. These will include undefended divorces, claims arising out of motor accidents, actions for debt (including hire-purchase debt), breach of contract, possession of land, disputes between landlord and tenant, wrongful dismissal by employers, negligent workmanship, race relations, most disputes between neighbours, trespass and assault (which is a civil action as well as a criminal offence).

In many cases, if more than £1,000 is in dispute or if land with a rateable value of over £1,000 per annum is involved, the county court has no jurisdiction unless both parties agree that the case should be heard there. It is sometimes advisable to agree to this. Costs are much lower than in the High Court, which is where the case would otherwise be heard.

Crown Courts

If a defendant is charged with a serious criminal offence, he will probably be committed to stand trial by jury in a crown court. Also, if anyone is dissatisfied with the outcome of criminal proceedings in a magistrates' court, he can usually appeal to a crown court either against conviction or sentence or both.

The crown courts were set up in many regional centres in 1972 in place of the old Quarter Sessions and Assizes. According to the importance of the case it will be before a High Court judge (sitting alone) or a circuit judge or recorder. Lay justices can also sit and hear cases with recorder or circuit judge.

The High Court

Cases where the amount of money involved is above the county court's limits may be heard in the High Court. This court also hears all defended divorces, as well as appeals from magistrates' courts in matrimonial cases. Occasionally on points of law it can also hear criminal appeals from magistrates' courts.

The High Court is divided into three divisions: the Queen's Bench Division, the Family Division and the Chancery Division. Each of these specialises in particular areas of the law.

The High Court is based in the Law Courts in the Strand. However, cases are also heard in the provinces at district registries.

The Court of Appeal

The Court of Appeal hears appeals from county courts, crown courts, and the High Court. In a criminal case, the Court of Appeal can quash the verdict, reduce the sentence or order a fresh trial. In a civil case, the court can reverse the decision, reduce or increase the amount of compensation originally awarded or order a fresh trial.

The House of Lords

The House of Lords is the supreme court of appeal. It hears appeals from the Court of Appeal, or, sometimes, direct from the High Court. The 'legal' House of Lords is comprised only of the 'law lords', who are the highest-ranking judges. The other peers by convention do not hear cases although they have the theoretical right to do so.

Tribunals

Apart from what may be called the conventional courts, there are many other tribunals with judicial powers. Some of these are of great practical importance. They include rent tribunals, industrial relations tribunals and the Lands Tribunal (which deals with compulsory purchase). The procedure before these is comparatively informal but legal representation is sometimes advisable.

The Legal Profession

Solicitors

Solicitors are the main link between the public and the law. There are over 20,000 solicitors in England and Wales. If a potential litigant needs the services of a solicitor for the first time, his choice is often guided by personal recommendation. If no solicitor is known to him he can contact the Law Society, which is the solicitors' professional body and which will supply a list of solicitors in his area. Alternatively, inquiries can be made at a local citizens' advice bureau.

There is a widespread reluctance to go to a solicitor among people who have not done so previously. However, it is usually advisable to consult a solicitor as soon as it is apparent that one has a legal problem. If not, one may say or do something which will jeopardise one's legal rights. For instance, it is a common error that if there is 'nothing in writing', one is not bound by a contract. This is often not true. Again, if one is contemplating buying a house, it is all too easy to write a letter which commits one to the purchase, whatever the usual legal and planning inquiries may subsequently reveal.

The relationship between a solicitor and his client may be summarised as follows:

A solicitor is bound to keep secret everything which his client tells him. Not even a court can make him break confidence.

A solicitor is not bound to believe in the justice of his clients' case or (in a criminal matter) in his innocence. However, he owes a duty to the court as well as to his client. He cannot make any statement which to his own certain knowledge is untrue. Therefore, for example, if his client tells him that he is guilty, he cannot continue with the case if the client wishes to plead not guilty.

A solicitor must keep detailed and separate accounts of any money which is entrusted to him by the client. These accounts are regularly audited.

The same firm of solicitors cannot usually act for both sides in the same matter, even if a different member of the firm acts for each client.

A solicitor is liable to his client if the client suffers loss through negligent advice. However, a solicitor is not guilty of negligence if, taking due care, he advises on a difficult or doubtful point of law and is subsequently proved wrong. All solicitors are heavily insured against such claims so that a client who has suffered loss in this way should be able to obtain full satisfaction.

If a client loses money through the dishonesty of a solicitor, or through his failure to account for money, the client may be able to obtain compensation from the Law Society's compensation fund.

If a client is dissatisfied with his solicitor for any reason whether it be inefficiency, overcharging or dishonesty, he should complain to the Law Society. To some extent, though, the Law Society's powers are limited. It cannot, for instance, order a solicitor to pay compensation. The Law Society will give further details of what it can and cannot do, upon request.

Barristers

There are about 3,000 barristers, most of them practising within the walls of the four ancient Inns of Court in London. Others work in provincial centres, eg Bristol, Cardiff and Manchester. Unlike solicitors, barristers cannot form partnerships, but a dozen or so will work together in a 'set of chambers', employing a clerk and typist in common. Often the 'head of chambers' will be a queen's counsel. A barrister is appointed a QC by the Lord Chancellor as a mark of his eminence and seniority. QCs are retained in important cases only and are always assisted in court by a junior barrister.

Most barristers are primarily advocates, ie they plead cases in court. But they also give a consultancy service. Some specialise in a particular branch of the law, such as crime or divorce. They are the only lawyers allowed to speak in some of the higher courts. Their work also includes giving 'counsel's opinion' to solicitors on some point of law or procedural tactics; they may advise in writing or in conference in their chambers.

Barristers have to be instructed through a solicitor. They cannot be approached directly. The only exception to this is the 'dock brief'. If a defendant in a criminal case in the crown court decides at the last moment that he wants to be legally represented he may ask any barrister who happens to be in court to act for him. Similarly, barristers' fees (other than those for a dock brief) are paid by the solicitor and will appear as separate items on his bill to his client. Barristers cannot sue for their fees. Conversely, they cannot be sued for negligence. This is because there is no legal contract between a barrister and his client. Strictly, a barrister agrees to act for nothing; his fees are a mere 'honorarium'. It is possible, however, that a barrister may be sued for negligence in 'non-contentious' work, such as writing an opinion on a taxation scheme.

Civil Cases

If a legal dispute can only be resolved by the judgement of a court, the solicitors on both sides will file with the court documents which are known as 'pleadings'. The solicitors acting for the claimant or plaintiff will file either particulars of a claim (in the county court) or a statement of claim (in the High Court). This is a statement of why the claim is brought and for what. Solicitors to the defendant will file a defence in answer to these. (This is a statement of why the claim should not succeed.) The purpose of pleadings is to set out the issues which the judge will have to try.

If either party to the case is not legally represented, he is known as a 'litigant in person' (see also p 14). In a county court case, printed forms are available at the court office for any litigant in person. These will enable him to set out his claim or his answer to a claim made against him.

Procedure at County Courts

The plaintiff's advocate will begin the proceedings by making a speech in which he explains his case to the judge. He then calls the evidence in support of his case. This evidence may take the form of the oral evidence of witnesses or documentary evidence, such as affidavits. As each witness is called, the defendant's advocate has the opportunity of cross-examining him and challenging his testimony. After all the evidence on behalf of the plaintiff has been called, the advocate for the defence then calls the evidence for his case, with the same opportunity for cross-examination by the plaintiff's advocate. After this come the closing speeches. The first is made by the defendant's advocate. The plaintiff's advocate has the last word.

High Court

The procedure in the High Court is the same as that in the county court except that the defendant's counsel has the opportunity of making an opening speech before calling his own evidence.

Criminal Proceedings

Magistrates' Court

If the defendant is pleading 'not guilty' the prosecution (which may be represented either by a lawyer or by a police officer) makes an opening speech and calls its evidence. The defence has the right to cross-examine the prosecution witnesses. After this, the defence may submit that the prosecution evidence is so inadequate that there is no case to answer. However, if the justices do not accept this submission, the trial must continue.

The defendant or his lawyer calls his evidence and then makes his speech. The magistrates then consider their verdict. If they find the defendant guilty, they then hear for the first time details of his past convictions. In many cases, the magistrates may wish to know more about the defendant's background. For example, they may want to know whether he is married and what are his means. The magistrates can then pass sentence. If in view of the defendant's past history they consider that their powers are inadequate, they can send him to the crown court for sentence.

If the defendant pleads guilty, the prosecution will outline the offence which is admitted. The court will also be told of the defendant's previous convictions. Again, details may also be required of the defendant's background. The defendant or his advocate can then make a 'plea in mitigation' which advances any reasons there may be for treating the defendant leniently. After this, the magistrates can either pass sentence or remit the defendant to the crown court.

Crown Courts

If the defendant pleads not guilty, a jury must be empanelled. The defendant has the right to object to up to seven jurors without giving any reason. (This is sometimes done so as to achieve a jury of one sex or of mixed sexes.) He can also challenge any other juror for 'good cause'. A good cause would be that the juror knows the defendant or is in some way prejudiced against him. The prosecution can ask a juror to 'stand by'. If it does so, the juror will only be included if there are not enough other jurors available to make up a full jury. Like the defence, the prosecution can challenge any juror for good cause. It is also possible for either the prosecution or the defence to challenge the whole group of potential jurors.

Counsel for the prosecution then makes the opening speech in which he informs the jury of the charges he intends to prove. He then calls his evidence. The defence can cross-examine the prosecution witnesses. At end of the prosecution case, the defence has the right to submit that there is no case to answer. If the judge does not accept this submission, the trial continues.

If counsel for the defence (or the defendant if he is unrepresented) is calling more than one witness about the facts of the case (as opposed to evidence concerning the defendant's character) he can make an opening speech. He next calls his evidence and the prosecution can cross-examine the defence witnesses. The prosecution and the defence then make their final speeches in that order. The judge sums up. He can at this point direct the jury to return a verdict of not guilty. If he does not do this, the jury retires to consider its verdict. If the defendant is found guilty, the judge is then told of his past convictions. The defence can make a plea in mitigation. The judge then passes sentence.

If the defendant pleads guilty, the prosecution briefly outlines the facts of the case to the judge and gives details of past convictions. The defence makes a plea in mitigation. After this, sentence is passed.

Litigants in Person

Every litigant has the right to conduct his own case without legal representation. Indeed, there are in certain areas courts known as 'small claims courts' which hear claims involving £75 and in which the cost of legal representation cannot be recovered from the unsuccessful party. 'Litigants in person' are rare outside the county courts and magistrates' courts, and even small county court cases can involve difficult points of law in which an unrepresented litigant will be at a disadvantage against a professional opponent. Cases which are most suited to litigants in person are those which turn largely on questions of fact rather than of law, such as minor traffic offences being tried in a magistrates' court.

How to Start Court Proceedings

Anyone who wishes to start court proceedings can find out the address of his local court from a telephone directory, his citizens' advice bureau, the town hall or the police station. In a county court case, the litigant will usually have to fill in the court forms which set out his case. These forms can be obtained from the court office. The defendant in court proceedings will be given details of when and where the court sits in a notice which will be served on him. In the High Court the notice is called a writ, in the county court a plaint, and in the magistrates' court a summons.

Conducting the Case

A person who is conducting his own case may have to arrange for witnesses to attend the court hearing. He must also bring any other evidence to court, such as notices to quit or receipts.

The court will help an unrepresented litigant to present his case properly and within the rules of procedure. The rules of evidence, for example, are extremely complicated and it is hard for a layman to conduct his case without infringing them occasionally. However, the following points should perhaps be borne particularly in mind:

Admissible evidence: it is essential that every witness who is called in support of the litigant's case can testify to everything relevant from his own first-hand knowledge. (This applies also to the litigant himself.)

Anything else is 'hearsay' and inadmissible. Thus it is useless for A to vouch for the truth of an event on the grounds that B had told him that he had seen it. B himself must be called.

Leading questions to one's own witnesses are forbidden. Leading questions are commonly defined as those which suggest the answers to them. For example, it would be a leading question for a petitioner in a divorce case to ask his witness: 'Did you see my wife commit adultery on 1 January?' However, it would not be a leading question to ask: 'Do you recall anything which happened on 1 January and if so, what?'

It would not be a leading question for the counsel for the wife in the same case to ask the alleged co-respondent: 'Did you commit adultery on 1 January?' This is because there is no attempt to prompt the witness unfairly and because the answer which is sought is 'no' and not 'yes'. There is no rule against leading questions in the cross-examination of a witness on the other side.

The Remedies Offered by the Courts

'No right without a remedy' is an ancient legal maxim. The courts have a variety of means by which they can enforce a subject's legal rights. The following are the main remedies:

Damages

Damages are a financial compensation which represents the loss which has been caused to a plaintiff through the fault of the defendant. Perhaps the simplest example of damages is that of 'liquidated damages'. These are the amount of any specific sum due to the plaintiff, for instance, under a debt. Naturally, damages can be awarded for any quantifiable financial loss. For example, A may agree to buy a car from B for £500 but then fail to honour his contract. B finds that he can sell the car for only £400 on the open market. B can therefore sue A for damages of £100.

Damages can also be awarded for 'pain and suffering'. For instance, a plaintiff can recover damages for personal injury on the grounds of loss of earnings and loss of 'amenities'. Obviously, it is extremely difficult to quantify such damages in terms of money. Nonetheless, this is precisely what the court has to do.

In order for a claim for damages to succeed, it must be shown that what was suffered by the plaintiff was caused directly (even if not immediately) by the act or omission of the defendant. Whether or not the claim will fail by reason of the 'remoteness' of the damage from the defendant's act will be a question of fact in every case. This principle in no way conflicts with the rule that 'one must take one's victim as one finds him'. For instance, if in a personal injury case the plaintiff, because of some pre-existing weakness (such as an 'eggshell skull'), suffers greater injury than the average man might have done, his damages will not be reduced on that account. However, under the principle of 'contributory negligence' they may be reduced if he was partly to blame.

Every plaintiff is under a duty to 'mitigate his damage'. In other words, he must take reasonable steps to ensure that he does not suffer more than is necessary from the defendant's act. As an illustration, if the plaintiff is suing the defendant for wrongfully dismissing him from his employment, he will in principle be able to obtain damages for his actual loss of earnings. But if he has made no serious effort to find new employment, his damages may be reduced.

Specific Performance

The courts try to give effect to the principle of full restitution. The ideal is to restore the plaintiff to his position before he was wronged. Sometimes, damages will not be an adequate remedy. The court may therefore give other remedies. Where there is a breach of contract, the court may enforce 'specific performance' of the contract.

For example, if there is a contract to buy a house the purchaser may not be truly compensated by a return of his deposit. There may be no substitute for the house which he particularly wished to live in. Therefore, he may obtain an order for specific performance. On the other hand, the vendor of the house stood to receive only cash had the contract been performed. Therefore, he can be fully compensated by damages and would not be able to require specific performance.

Specific performance is never enforced to make someone carry out a contract of personal service, such as making an actor fulfil his engagement.

Injunctions

Injunctions are a form of order which can be issued by the High Court or by the county court (although the latter will only do so as an ancillary remedy to a money claim). Most injunctions are 'prohibitory'. These prevent a person against whom they are issued from carrying out or continuing the action to which there is an objection. An example of this is an injunction to prevent a husband from molesting his wife. However, some injunctions are 'mandatory'. These actually order someone to do something. It is more difficult to obtain a mandatory than a prohibitive injunction.

As with specific performance, the courts are reluctant to grant an injunction where damages would be an adequate remedy—though this rule is not inflexible. For example, if someone were causing a nuisance to his neighbours, it would be unfair to allow him to continue doing so merely because he was well able to afford any damages which were awarded against him. To take another example, the beneficiaries of a trust can apply to the court for an injunction to prevent the trustee from making an improvident sale of trust property, even though they would have a claim for damages against him were he to do so.

In some cases, the plaintiff in a court action needs a legal remedy urgently. By the time his case comes to court, the damage which he will suffer may be irremediable. Where the court is satisfied that his case has at least a reasonable chance of ultimate success and that the situation is sufficiently grave, it may order an interim or 'interlocutory' injunction against the defendant. This will maintain the status quo until the action is heard.

Restitution of Property

If property is being wrongfully retained, the court can order its return to the true owner. Similarly, the court can grant possession of land to the person entitled to it.

Prerogative Orders

The High Court often has the power to intervene when a lower court or tribunal or any other body such as a government department offends against the rules of 'natural justice'. (In this context, the phrase has a fairly restricted and well-defined meaning.) The court intervenes by the issue of 'prerogative orders', which will set aside the offending action. A prerogative order might be issued where a person has been disciplined by his trade union or professional body without being given a fair hearing. Another example might be where someone has been judged by a magistrate who had a personal interest in his case.

Limitation Periods

The law lays down maximum periods within which a legal action may be brought. When these periods expire, any rights which a potential plaintiff might have had are extinguished. Therefore, it is essential that an action be begun (ie that a writ or plaint be issued) before the end of the relevant period. In outline, 'limitation periods' are as follows:

For most actions for breaking a contract or for other wrongs (ie nuisance, negligence): six years.

For actions involving claims for personal injuries: three years.

For actions for breach of certain kinds of contract (including contracts under seal (see p 91)): twelve years.

For actions for possession of land (eg evicting squatters): twelve years.

In general, these periods are calculated from the date when the right to bring a court action arose. For instance, in a contract case, the period runs from the date of the breach of contract. In certain other cases, where damage has to be suffered before an action can be brought, the period will run from the date of the damage. If there is a continuing wrong (for example, noisy neighbours) the plaintiff can still bring an action, although he will not be entitled to damages in relation to anything which happened before the beginning of the relevant limitation period.

Exceptions

There are exceptions to the limitation periods. For instance, if the plaintiff was a minor at the time of the wrong, the period will not begin against him until he comes of age. Again, if the defendant has concealed his wrong-doing, time will not begin to run until the plaintiff discovers it (or ought to have discovered it). In personal injury actions, the three-year limitation period runs from the date on which the plaintiff first knew all four of the following:

1 That the injury was significant
2 That the injury was caused wholly or partly by the fault of the defendant
3 The identity of the defendant.
4 If the act or omission in question was that of someone other than the defendant, the identity of such person and the grounds on which an action against the defendant could be brought.

For example, if an employee contracts an industrial disease which does not manifest itself for some years, he may have three years from the discovery of the disease to sue his employers.

In personal injury cases, the court has power to disregard the limitation periods altogether. It has no such power in other cases.

Actions for such remedies as specific performance or injunctions are not always subject to the limitation periods (although the court may apply the periods to them), but they are subject to the rule of equity that a plaintiff must not 'sleep upon his rights'. Therefore, if the court considers that there has been an unreasonable delay in bringing the case, it will dismiss it. Naturally, what constitutes a reasonable time depends upon the facts of each case.

Costs in Civil Cases

For any litigant who is not eligible for legal aid, the cost of a court action is an important factor in deciding whether to commence and whether to continue with his case. It is impossible to give any guide to how much any particular kind of case might cost. This will vary enormously from case to case. A solicitor may be able to give a rough estimate before litigation is embarked upon but he cannot foresee how the case may develop. To take an extreme example, a case which begins in a county court could go on to the Court of Appeal.

As a general rule, 'costs follow the event'. This means that the losing party will have to pay the costs of the winner, as well as his own costs. However, the court will only award to the winner such costs as it considers reasonable. The costs will be assessed by an official of the court (the registrar in the county court and the taxing master in the High Court). The court scrutinises the bill of costs very carefully and it may be that a successful litigant will not recover the full amount which he has expended. In every case, the award of costs is in the discretion of the court. However, a successful litigant is in general unable to recover costs from a legally aided opponent.

Payments into Court

A defendant may pay to the court a sum in satisfaction of the plaintiff's claim against him. This amount need not be the full amount of the sum claimed or, where no specific sum is claimed, as much as the plaintiff is expecting to obtain. The 'payment-in' presents the plaintiff with a dilemma. He may accept it, and if he does so, he will usually be awarded any costs which he may have incurred at that stage. If he rejects the payment-in but ultimately recovers in damages a smaller amount, he will usually have to bear both his and his opponents' costs. This problem may be particularly acute in a personal injuries action, where it is often hard to forecast the amount of compensation which the plaintiff will receive. However, the system of 'payments-in' has the great advantage of discouraging needless litigation.

Legal Aid

In some cases legal advice and assistance can be obtained and court proceedings undertaken, the expense of which is borne out of public funds.

A distinction may be drawn between the Legal Advice and Assistance Scheme, which was introduced in 1973, and legal aid for litigation. Under the Legal Advice and Assistance Scheme there is a minimum of formality. The applicant simply goes to a solicitor who is on the scheme and gives him details of his means. The solicitor will say whether he is eligible and will deal with the paperwork himself. Many firms of solicitors operate the scheme. A list can be obtained from any citizens' advice bureau or from the local law society.

This scheme offers not only oral advice from a solicitor but also correspondence and negotiations in legal matters on behalf of the client. Moreover, legal documents (such as wills) can be drawn up under the scheme. It is also possible for conveyancing to be carried out. Advice can be given on what action the client should take in proceedings before a court but the solicitor cannot take any such action himself. If the client has a case which is to go before a tribunal (for instance, for redundancy payments) the solicitor can prepare a case in writing for the use of the client. However, the scheme will not cover the solicitor's costs if he represents the client at the hearing before the tribunal.

Financial Limits

A person's right to free legal advice and assistance from a solicitor depends upon what is known as his 'disposable' capital and his 'disposable' income.

Disposable Capital

The applicant's disposable capital is basically his net free capital. In the calculation of this, the applicant's personal and household effects and any tools of his trade are ignored. The value of his house (after deducting any mortgage) can be relevant but is usually excluded.

Disposable Income

This is the total income from all sources, less deductions under two heads. The first head is statutory deductions, such as income tax and national insurance contributions. The second head is the allowances for dependants.

Revision of Rates

The levels of disposable income and capital below which you are entitled to legal advice and assistance and the amounts of any contributions which you may have to pay are frequently changed. Your solicitor will advise you if you are eligible.

Legal Aid for Court Proceedings

Legal aid is administered by local committees of the Law Society, composed of solicitors and barristers. In civil cases, you apply to them for the issue of a certificate, which they will grant unless they consider that you have no case at all. (If you are refused a certificate, you have a right of appeal to the area committee.) If you do not have a solicitor you can obtain the application form from the local citizens' advice bureau, the court office or the committee itself. After the certificate is issued you have twenty-eight days to choose a solicitor from the legal aid panel.

The financial limits for civil court proceedings are similar (but not identical) to those for legal advice and assistance. The applicant will be advised by his solicitor whether he is eligible and, if so, how much contribution he will have to make.

The legal aid system in criminal cases is different. Legal aid can be granted immediately by the court, although a means test will follow and the recipient of the legal aid may have to make repayments.

2 Marriage and the Family

The Legal Nature of Marriage

The House of Lords has defined marriage as 'the voluntary union for life of one man and one woman to the exclusion of all others'.

Who May Marry

The parties to a marriage must be single and of opposite sexes. There is no such thing as a homosexual marriage.

Bigamous Marriages

In the past bigamy was a serious offence, often resulting in a long prison sentence. Today the maximum penalty is still seven years' imprisonment, but in practice the authorities tend towards leniency unless the motive for the second marriage is financial gain. Recognised defences to the charge of bigamy include:

A bona fide belief in the death of one's partner.

His or her continued absence for seven years, provided there is no reason to believe he or she is still alive.

Marriage under Eighteen

No one may marry under the age of sixteen. Between sixteen and eighteen a person may marry with parental consent. If parents are divorced, only the parent who has been granted legal custody need give consent.

Parents can give their consent either on a form supplied by the registrar or by sending a letter signed by each of them. In the event of either parent opposing the marriage, the minor has the right to ask the court to override the parent's refusal. Consent may then be given by a judge in the local county court, but more usually the minor goes to the local magistrates' court, where the magistrates hear the case in private. It is not necessary, but it may be helpful, to have a lawyer question the parents about the true reasons for their opposition. There is no risk of publicity.

The decision of the magistrates is final. A disappointed minor cannot appeal.

Under Scottish law parental consent is not required, provided the strict residence qualification is met.

Marriage to Foreigners

So far as English law is concerned, an Englishwoman who marries a foreigner does not lose her citizenship of the UK. But the law of her husband's country could compel her to renounce it.

A woman from a country outside the UK who marries an Englishman is entitled to become a UK citizen by registering with the Nationality Division of the Home Office. It is more complicated for a foreign man who marries an Englishwoman to become a citizen of the UK. He must apply for naturalisation.

Breaking Off an Engagement

Since 1970 a woman can no longer claim damages if the man who promised to marry her changes his mind. She will have no legal redress, even if she has travelled many thousands of miles to marry her fiancé; she has ceased to work; or she has spent her money buying furniture or household effects in expectation of their setting up home together.

However, she will be able to keep the engagement ring even if *she* breaks off the engagement. The man could only claim it back in the rare circumstance of it being a family heirloom.

All other engagement presents must usually be given back if the marriage is cancelled, whoever breaks it off.

Obligations of Marriage

Sexual Rights

A married woman, by implication, consents to sexual intercourse with her husband. So long as they are living together and she consents he cannot be guilty of rape, although he can be convicted of assault if he uses force. A wife can end her husband's right to sexual intercourse by getting a divorce or a decree of judicial separation from the

Family Division of the High Court, or a separation order from the local magistrates' court. She can also withdraw her consent by a separation agreement, particularly one containing a non-molestation clause. If so, he could be convicted of rape.

Husband's Right to Locate Family Home

Usually the husband will in practice decide where the family home should be. This is because he is responsible for the financial support of his family and will wish to live where he can find work. The court cannot order a wife to live with her husband, but if she unreasonably refuses to accompany him to a new home, it can declare her to be in desertion.

Wife's Right to Husband's Surname

A married woman has the right to use her husband's surname and to continue to use it even after divorce—though not for the purpose of defrauding him.

Duty of Loyalty

The law imposes a duty on both husband and wife to keep each other's secrets. Even after divorce their duty of loyalty to each other must be respected. Neither may later divulge confidences obtained during their marriage. For example, if the wife of a famous man wishes to tell the story of their married life to the newspapers, the court is able to forbid her to publish an account of her husband's personal affairs, or reveal what he did in private during their marriage.

Giving Evidence against Each Other

In a civil trial, a husband or wife may refuse to answer questions if the answer might imply that the other has been guilty of a crime. In a criminal case neither husband nor wife can be compelled to give evidence against the other. But where a husband or wife wishes to give evidence against the other in a criminal trial, the jury is entitled to hear it. A spouse would be obliged to give evidence against the other only where he had committed a crime against her (or she against him).

The Right to Sue

There is nothing to prevent a husband suing his wife, or vice versa. For example, a husband who is injured in a car which his wife is driving would have a claim against her if she was driving carelessly. (In practice, the claim would be met by the insurance company.)

Who Owns the Home?

House in Husband's Name Only

Where the family home is in the husband's name alone, on divorce the judge can order the husband to transfer it to his wife. The fact that he has paid for it does not necessarily mean that he can keep it, particularly if his wife and family have nowhere else to live. The husband will normally be deprived of his house until his children have grown up.

House in Wife's Name Only

What is the position if the husband pays for a house but puts it in his wife's name only? Here a judge was at one time bound to infer that the husband intended to make his wife a gift of the house, but in recent years, with increasing equality of the sexes, there is no longer an overriding presumption of gift in favour of the wife.

The Family Home

Many couples nowadays buy their home in both names. An important advantage of co-ownership is that if they separate and the house is sold, the proceeds of the sale can normally be divided equally.

Co-ownership—Joint or In Common

When a husband and wife buy their house together, their lawyer will ask them whether they wish to own it either jointly or in common. One reason for making this distinction is that it determines who will inherit the other's half share if one of them dies unexpectedly.

Joint ownership is generally preferable because it allows the wife to inherit her husband's half share automatically on his death. Similarly, the wife's half share will pass to her husband if she dies first. Whatever property is owned jointly, the survivor becomes sole owner of the whole property. It cannot be left to a third party by the will of a joint owner when he dies.

Ownership in common means ownership in separate shares. This would be useful for a woman who has children by an earlier marriage. She will be able to leave her half share of the house to them in her will. Again, a husband and wife may wish to be strictly businesslike about the division of their property. If, for instance, on buying a house costing £20,000, the husband provides £5,000 of the purchase money and the wife £15,000, their deed of ownership could state explicitly that their respective shares are one quarter and three-quarters. On the other hand, a woman who anticipates outliving her husband would be wise to insist on having their house owned jointly, since she will then become sole owner on his death by survivorship.

Converting 'Joint' to 'In Common'

Any joint owner can take steps to convert the joint ownership into ownership in common. One owner sends to the other written notice to 'sever' the joint ownership. The notice terminates the right of inheritance by survivorship. It is best done through a solicitor.

The Family Home

Protecting Wife's Rights of Occupation

If her husband's behaviour has driven a wife out of the family home, a judge can turn the tables on him by ordering him out and allowing the wife back in. The judge can also make an order restraining him from molesting his wife on pain of imprisonment.

Benefits of Registration

Naturally where the family home is owned by her husband the wife may worry in case he should sell it. To prevent this, Parliament has given wives the legal right to stay in the family home. But a wife *must* protect this right by registration at the Land Registry. (This is a simple matter but it is best entrusted to a solicitor.) Once she has registered, anyone buying the house from her husband cannot evict her. In practice any prospective buyer acting with reasonable care is bound to find out that she is registered; he is then likely to refuse to buy the house. This could place the husband in an awkward position (see Chapter 6).

The wife does not have to wait until trouble has started between herself and her husband. She can register at any time, and without her husband necessarily finding out—though the husband's solicitors would be able to find out if they made inquiries at the Land Registry.

A wife who delays registration faces certain dangers. For example, a wily husband may be able to finalise the sale of the house and pocket the proceeds before her registration has gone through.

Her solicitor should advise her about her right to register and should also stress the importance of registering promptly. She might later sue him for carelessness if, as a result of his delay, she lost her home.

Disputes over Family Assets

If a husband parts from his wife, he should leave her with sufficient furniture and household utensils to live in reasonable comfort. In practice it can be difficult to decide who owns the household goods and the court can be asked to settle disputes when a couple separate. The overriding principle is that ownership depends on the original intention of whoever bought the item. There are a number of legal rules for deciding who owns what:

Wedding presents from relatives or friends of the husband belong to him; wedding presents from the wife's friends or relatives belong to her.

Any item bought out of savings from housekeeping will belong to them jointly.

A couple often open a joint bank account to meet household expenditure. Any asset bought out of a joint bank account is not necessarily owned equally.

Trial Marriages

In anticipation of getting married a couple may buy furniture and rent or buy a flat together. If the engagement is broken off they can ask the court to decide any disputes about ownership. The judge would resolve their dispute in the same way as if they had been married and then separated.

Gifts between Husband and Wife

A husband or wife who makes a gift to the other cannot later claim it back in the event of divorce. The only exception is where a domineering husband extracts a large sum of money or substantial assets from his wife. If the judge considers that he exercised 'undue influence' over her, she (or her family if she dies) will be entitled to have the gift returned. The same could apply where a weak-willed husband gives all his money to a domineering wife, but 'undue influence' would be more difficult to prove in this case, because the law tends to presume that any gift made by a husband to his wife was given willingly.

When the Husband Goes Bankrupt

A husband engaged in a speculative business may try to protect certain family possessions by transferring them to his wife. The transfer is valid as between himself and his wife, but third persons to whom he owes money may be able to prove that he gave assets to his wife in order to prevent creditors from claiming them. In this event, the creditors will be entitled to insist that the wife gives up the assets.

Family Insurance

Taking Out a Policy on the Other's Life

A wife has an insurable interest in her husband's life. Similarly, a husband may take out a policy of insurance for any amount on the life of his wife. On her death he can claim the full amount due under the policy. He does not have to prove that he actually sustained any financial loss by reason of her death.

The law also allows special advantages to both husbands and wives in respect of insurance benefits. Since 1882 it has been possible for a husband to take out an insurance policy on his own life in favour of his wife or children. (A wife, too, can insure her own life for the benefit of her husband or children.) The practical advantages of this type of policy are:

Even if the husband dies in debt, the money received cannot be claimed by his creditors.

His wife and children are entitled to be paid the money due under the policy immediately he dies. All they need to do is to present the death certificate.

The sum insured is free of capital transfer tax so long as the premiums were part of his 'normal expenditure'.

During his lifetime the person insured receives tax relief on the premiums.

Damages for Fatal Accidents

Should a husband or wife be killed in an accident, the person responsible will have to pay substantial damages. Any relative who was financially dependent on the deceased has a claim, not only the surviving spouse but also children and parents. Any relative who received financial support from the deceased can make a separate claim for damages. Although the 'common law' wife or mistress of the deceased has no right to claim, illegitimate children of the deceased are entitled to compensation.

Whilst grief or mental suffering alone is no ground for a claim, a loss need not be measurable solely in cash. Where the wife has been killed, the husband may claim for the loss of her services and for any resulting increase in his expenses. To assess the amount of damages, the judge will estimate the relative's approximate annual cash loss and multiply this amount by up to sixteen years to arrive at a capital sum. The fact that a widow decides to go out to work after her husband's death does not affect the amount she can claim. She is entitled to be restored to the financial position she was in when her husband was alive. The income of the deceased must be held to have been his legitimate income. In one case where it was proved that the income of her husband had come from his criminal activities, his widow was allowed nothing for his death.

There is a three-year time limit for taking legal action which is usually brought by the personal representative of the deceased on behalf of all dependants. If he fails to start a court action within six months after death, each dependant may start legal proceedings himself.

Marriage and Wills

Marriage automatically cancels any prior will so anyone who gets married should arrange to make a new will. If a new will is not made the surviving husband or wife will inherit the first share in the event of the other's death. After this the remaining assets will go to the other next of kin in a rigid order of priority laid down by the law (see Chapter 5). Any special provision for, say, a distant relative or a child by an earlier marriage, must be made by means of a new will.

3 Maintenance and Divorce

Duty of Husband to Maintain Wife

In marriage it is generally the husband's duty to provide financially for his wife and family. Only in exceptional circumstances could a wife be under a duty to maintain her husband.

Any money a wife may earn herself is hers to spend as she pleases. While living with her husband, a woman has no right to a fixed share of his income, nor any right to know how much he earns. If he gives her too little money for the needs of her family, she cannot compel him to give her more. Nevertheless:

She could use his meanness as a ground for divorce, claiming that his failure to provide her with adequate means has caused the breakdown of their marriage.

While living with him she is entitled to buy domestic items such as food and clothing on credit in his name. Her husband will be obliged to pay, unless he has previously told shopkeepers not to give her credit.

Once she has separated from her husband, she is no longer entitled to obtain goods on credit in his name. Her best course is to go to the magistrates' court and ask for an order for maintenance.

Even though they may be living in the same house, she can still ask for maintenance if 'cohabitation' has ceased, ie they are no longer living as husband and wife in the true sense, and he has neglected to maintain her. (A wife's rights over the family home are discussed in Chapter 2.)

Social Security

Meantime, she can apply to an office of the Department of Health & Social Security for benefits to live on. The department will allow her enough money for food and household essentials; the department will also pay the rent. If there is a mortgage, the department will pay instalments of mortgage interest in order to prevent the building society cancelling the mortgage and selling her house. However, it will not pay instalments of capital. A wife who cannot keep up the full instalments should notify the building society at once of her position. If satisfied that there is no wilful default on her part, they will agree to accept only the interest due on the loan.

Where a husband neglects his wife so that she is obliged to get social security, the department can later insist on being repaid by him. Similarly, a wife whose husband is incapacitated could find the department making a claim against her. This may happen if, for example, she has means but has forced her husband to live on social security.

A husband whose earning capacity is impaired by illness could be entitled to be maintained by his wife. Her liability to pay would naturally depend on her resources.

Getting a Maintenance Order

The advantages of applying to the magistrates are simplicity, cheapness and speed. They have no power to grant the wife a divorce; this is dealt with by the Family Division of the High Court. But otherwise the magistrates have virtually the same powers as the Family Division.

How Much Maintenance?

There is no limit, in theory, to how much maintenance the magistrates can order in a wife's favour. As a rough guide, she can expect to be allowed one-third of her husband's earnings, assuming there are no children and she is not at work. If she too is earning, she should get one-third of their combined earnings, and an additional sum for each child.

To take out a summons for maintenance in the magistrates' court, the wife can go to her local court any day at 10am and tell the office that she wants to do so. She will then be taken to see the magistrate (or sometimes the chief clerk). All she need tell him is that her husband has failed to provide maintenance for herself or her children. She will then be given a date when she must return to court for her complaint to be heard. She need pay no fee and in the meantime a court official will serve a summons on her husband for him to appear at court on the same date.

Legal Advice and the Magistrates' Court

Although a lawyer is not essential, the assistance of a solicitor is desirable to protect a wife's interests. He can speak for her in court and conduct necessary dealings with her husband. If her husband disputes her right to maintenance and she has no solicitor, she can ask the court to adjourn the case to enable her to get legal assistance. The court office will tell her about solicitors near the court or near her home. She is always entitled to have free legal aid and advice if she is hard up. (See Chapter 1 for a full account.)

When the Magistrates' Court Can Make an Order

The situation that most commonly results in an order being made for the husband to maintain his wife is where she complains that he has wilfully neglected her needs, or the needs of any of their children. The husband is obliged to give his wife a reasonable sum for housekeeping. The more he earns, the more the magistrates might expect him to provide for his family.

A number of other legal grounds, if proved, will enable the magistrates to order maintenance. These include desertion, adultery, cruelty or beating, sexual offences, compelling prostitution, having a venereal disease, persistent drunkenness, and drug addiction.

All these matters can involve legal complications, and the wife would be well advised to get legal representation, particularly as confirmation of such a complaint would normally be an essential step to getting a divorce.

Obstacles to Obtaining Maintenance

A wife does not automatically qualify for maintenance:

In the case of specific offences, such as cruelty, or adultery, she must apply to the magistrates within six months of its occurrence. However, a complaint of desertion or wilful neglect to maintain is considered to be a 'continuing' offence and there is no time limit.

The wife is not entitled to an order for maintenance if it is proved she has been guilty of adultery, unless her husband has condoned it. Condoning her adultery would mean having her back after he had found out about it and their continuing to live together.

If the wife herself has committed adultery, she ought to seek legal advice. Her solicitor may advise her to apply at once for a divorce in the Family Division, where she will be able to get maintenance unless her conduct has been 'outrageous'. Once divorce proceedings have been started by either party, the magistrates' court will refuse to hear an application for maintenance.

Scope of Magistrates' Powers

The magistrates' court is a domestic court and hears all cases in private. There is no risk of publicity. Once satisfied that a complaint has been made out, the magistrates can make an order that the wife is no longer bound to 'cohabit' with her husband. Although this amounts to a legal separation, it is not final and the parties can still come together again.

The magistrates can also order the husband to pay his wife any amount they think reasonable, taking into account his earning capacity and outgoings. For example, if he has two homes to run, both may have to suffer some reduction in living standards, but the court will not allow an innocent wife to be relegated to a lower standard of living than her husband.

The magistrates can also decide which parent is to have custody of the children, and can allow the other parent access to see them regularly.

In cases where the husband, say, comes to court, and asks for an adjournment in order to obtain legal advice, the court has the power to make an interim order for maintenance, for the time being (up to three months).

Compelling the Husband to Pay Maintenance

1 *Attachment of Earnings Order.* Where the husband has a steady job and is not likely to change it, the wife can ask the magistrate to order his employers to deduct the amount ordered from his salary and pay it into court, where she can collect it. This method of compelling payment is not much use where the husband can change his job frequently.

2 *Committal to Prison.* Alternatively, if he does not pay, the wife can ask the court to summon him for inquiry into his means, and his reasons for non-payment. If the magistrates are satisfied that he has the means to pay, they can compel payment under threat of imprisonment. In an average year about 3,000 men are committed to prison for failing to pay under maintenance orders.

Obtaining a Divorce

Application for a divorce can be made either to a local county court, or, in London, to the Divorce Registry at Somerset House, Strand, WC2R 1LP.

Do-It-Yourself Divorces

It is now possible to get a divorce without going before a judge provided there are no children. A court hearing must still take place if there are children of the marriage still under the age of sixteen (or eighteen if undergoing full-time schooling or training).

This new procedure where no hearing takes place applies only to divorce on the following grounds:

1 *Two years' separation*, provided the other partner notifies the court that he or she consents.

2 *Adultery*, provided that both partner and co-respondent notify the court that they do not intend to defend. (In addition a letter from each admitting their adultery would be the best proof to get.)

3 *Two years' desertion*, provided the partner notifies the court he or she does not intend to defend.

4 *Five years' separation*, provided the partner notifies the court he or she does not intend to defend.

The Petition

The person seeking a divorce is referred to as the petitioner, and the legal document that starts the ball rolling is called the petition. Three copies of the standard form are needed.

The next step is to take these forms together with a copy of the marriage certificate and the fee to the nearest county court office (most towns have divorce jurisdiction) or, if you live in London, direct to the Divorce Registry at Somerset House, The Strand, WC2R 1LP. The spouse seeking the divorce refers to the other on the form as 'the respondent', giving his full name and address and other details, including the address at which they last lived together.

The court office requires two completed copies of the petition, each duly signed by the petitioner, one of which it sends by post to her husband together with a form of receipt called an acknowledgement of service. He must sign this receipt and return it to the court office. On it he confirms he has received a copy of the petition and also that he consents to the divorce being granted. The court then sends the wife a copy of this acknowledgement of service and a week later she can go to the court office and complete another form called 'directions for trial'.

The Questionnaire

The petitioner will be asked to complete a detailed questionnaire, called an affidavit. Here again the court clerks will help, short of giving actual legal advice. The questionnaire repeats most of the information already given in the petition. It asks the petitioner to state the date of separation, brief reasons for it and also 'When and in what circumstances did you come to the conclusion that the marriage was in fact at an end?' This could be answered for example by saying: 'In June 1976 when he stopped telephoning me at weekends', or alternatively: 'In June 1976 when I got a letter telling me he had found another woman.' The answer to this question could be crucial because from it the judge will have to decide whether he considers the marriage has broken down irretrievably.

The questionnaire asks, too, the dates, places and periods of the petitioner's residence since separation (except in the case of adultery). It ends with an affidavit, which the petitioner signs and declares is true before a clerk at the court office. After the questionnaire has been handed in, it will be considered by the registrar of the court. In cases proceeding at the Divorce Registry, if the petitioner is prepared to wait, it is possible to ask for this consideration to take place straight away, in which event the petitioner will be referred to the registrar on duty for the day. He will be able to say at once whether the documents are satisfactory. In other cases, the registrar will consider the documents as soon as possible, and send notice to the petitioner if any point requires further explanation.

Decree Nisi and Decree Absolute

Although both husband and wife are notified in due course on what date their case will be placed before the judge, neither need attend. If all papers are in order, he will mark the petition 'decree nisi granted'. This means that six weeks later she can ask for the divorce to be made final. The final decree is called the 'decree absolute'.

To apply for the decree absolute, the petitioner must return to the court office after six weeks and fill in a further form. Until the divorce decree is made absolute, they are still legally married. Once the decree absolute is granted, the marriage is dissolved and either partner is free to marry again.

Financial Aspects of Divorce

The only snag about getting a do-it-yourself divorce is that the wife will not have any general legal advice about her financial rights. These days, the most important aspect of divorce from the wife's point of view is the financial provision to which she may be entitled. She may be entitled to periodical payments for maintenance and/or a share in the family assets. The law has changed in recent years and each case is considered individually, with few hard and fast rules. The danger for a wife who lets a divorce go through without getting legal advice is that ultimately she could lose financially.

Grounds for Divorce

Anyone who marries, and finds it was a mistake, must normally stay married for at least three years. Only in two situations can a judge allow a divorce within the three-year period. These are:

Exceptional Hardship. Where the person seeking the divorce, for example the wife, is suffering exceptional hardship through the continuance of the marriage, the judge could allow her to present a divorce petition immediately.

Exceptional Depravity. Where the other partner has behaved with exceptional depravity, the three-year waiting period may be dispensed with. This could apply, for example, if the husband commits a crime and is sent to prison within a few weeks of the marriage, or if from the start the other partner behaves in a highly promiscuous manner.

Even though the judge does not think the case serious enough to allow a divorce within the three-year period, he may still order the husband to pay his wife maintenance.

Irretrievable Breakdown of the Marriage

Since the Divorce Reform Act abolished the concept of marital 'crime' in 1971, the judge need only consider one basic question: 'Has the marriage broken down irretrievably?'

The petitioning party can prove the breakdown of the marriage in one of five ways:

Adultery
Intolerable behaviour
Desertion
Living apart for two years (if the partner consents)
Living apart for five years (without his or her consent)

Adultery

Under the old law, a single act of adultery was sufficient to bring the marriage to an end. Today the petitioner must prove not only that the other party has committed adultery, but also that he or she cannot tolerate living with the other.

Adultery is normally proved by obtaining a written confession from the other party. The petitioner's solicitors usually employ an inquiry agent for this purpose, since he will have the necessary experience in such matters. Alternatively, a simple letter of confession would be sufficient.

In the past, when a husband sought a divorce on the ground of his wife's adultery, he was entitled to obtain heavy damages against the man who committed adultery with his wife. In 1970 this right to damages was abolished, though the guilty man can still be ordered to pay the legal costs of the divorce.

Intolerable Behaviour

Complaining of the other party's intolerable behaviour is another way of proving that the marriage has broken down irretrievably. Under the new law it is not necessary to show that the other party's behaviour has affected the petitioner's health. He or she need only show that because of the other party's behaviour it is unreasonable to be expected to continue living with her or him.

Desertion

Here the petitioner can show that the marriage has broken down irretrievably because he or she has been deserted for a continuous period of two years. Desertion means that the other party has left the petitioner without reasonable excuse and with the obvious intention of ending the marriage. Thus, where the couple *agree to a separation*, neither is guilty of desertion and no divorce can be had on this ground.

The law relating to desertion is complicated. For example, if the couple resume cohabitation during the two-year period for a short time (less than six months) in the hope of reconciliation, this period does not count as part of the two-year desertion period, but only interrupts it; the period continues to run from the original date of desertion.

On the other hand, in the eyes of the law it is not always the party who actually leaves who is in desertion. It may be the conduct of the other which has driven him or her away. This is usually referred to as 'constructive' desertion and has the same effect as actual desertion.

Moving Home

Generally it is the duty of the wife to live with her husband, so she may be in desertion if she refuses to go with him to live in another part of the country, or even abroad. Although the husband has no absolute right to decide where they should live, she must not obstruct him unreasonably if the move will enable him to get a better job or further his career.

Request to Return

A husband or wife who has deserted the other can bring the desertion to an end by making a genuine request to return. This may have the effect of turning the tables. Thus, if a wife, for example, refuses to have her husband back without good reason after he has made an offer to return, the judge *may* consider that by refusing reconciliation *she* is in desertion.

Making regular payments of maintenance has no effect on desertion. A husband who refuses to return to live with his wife can be guilty of desertion even though he maintains her and the family. In practice, proof of desertion can be difficult since it invariably involves proving that the other party was acting unreasonably. It may be wiser to rely on the next, much simpler ground of separation (see below).

Divorce after Two Years' Separation

Provided the other party gives his or her written consent to the divorce, the petitioner needs only to prove that they have been living apart for two years or more. If, in the meantime, they have come together for *short* periods (less than six months), these periods of reconciliation do not count towards the two years, but otherwise incur no penalty. The key to getting a divorce after two years' separation is to obtain the other party's written consent. If this consent is refused, the petitioner may have to wait a further three years (see below).

Divorce after Five Years' Continuous Separation

On this ground, the consent of the partner is not necessary, and the marriage may be dissolved against the other's will.

This ground would be available where the other partner is in a mental institution, and cannot give consent to the divorce.

Short periods of reconciliation (less than six months) do not cancel previous periods of separation but they must be deducted when computing the overall five-year period.

Custody of the Children

When the wife obtains her divorce decree nisi, her lawyer can ask the judge also to confirm any arrangements with her husband about the children, maintenance, etc, which they have been able previously to agree. Should there be any dispute about the children, the house, or financial matters, the judge or registrar will hear the dispute at a later date in private.

The mother is almost invariably given the custody, particularly of young children and girls, and older children too are usually left with the mother. In deciding which parent is to have custody, it is the welfare of the child which is paramount. If the child is old enough, the judge may ask him or her with which parent he or she wishes to live. If in doubt, the judge can ask a welfare officer to visit the home of each parent and make a report.

Care and Control

Usually, the parent who is granted legal custody of the children is also the one who is entitled to look after them in fact. However, if he wishes, the judge may allow the wife the care and control of her children, which means they can live with her, but he may grant her husband their legal custody. In practice, this means that the father must be consulted before any important decision is made which affects the welfare or education of any of his children.

Access

This refers to the right of a parent to see his or her children regularly. Sometimes the parent who has the children may try to impede the other having access. In the event of a dispute, a disgruntled parent may ask the court to define the access arrangements and make an appropriate order. A judge might be persuaded in exceptional circumstances to disallow access altogether if he were satisfied that the parent in question possessed such a low moral character that contact was likely to harm the child's development.

Financial Arrangements

Provision for a Wife

In the average case, a wife may expect to receive about one-third of their combined incomes. For example, where she is earning nothing and her husband earns £3,000 a year, she will probably be allowed about £1,000. If she is already earning £600 a year herself, this will bring their total income to £3,600. Therefore, she will probably be entitled to about £600 from her husband bringing her total income up to £1,200. However, the 'one-third' device is purely a rule-of-thumb method and would have little influence where, for example, there are many children.

It may be that the wife has a good job and is not in financial need at the time of the divorce. Nevertheless, she should ask for maintenance in her petition. If she subsequently falls on hard times she can then come back to the court and ask for periodical payments. Similarly, she can apply for an increase if her own income is reduced, or her ex-husband's increases dramatically.

Agreed Maintenance

Usually, the petitioner's lawyers will be able to agree with those acting for the other party the amount of maintenance that should be paid. But if they cannot agree, the judge or registrar of the court will settle the amount in a private hearing. Both parties will have to submit a full statement of their financial affairs. If either party conceals his or her true financial position, he or she could be prosecuted.

In deciding the amount of maintenance, the registrar will take in to consideration a number of factors beside the actual income and financial resources of each. As far as possible he will try to place the wife in the same financial position she would have been in if her marriage had not broken down. If she has young children, their needs will be given priority. In practice, both she and her husband will usually have to face some decrease in their living standards.

One consideration affecting the amount of maintenance is the length of the marriage. A woman who is young and able to work cannot regard her ex-husband as a ready source of income for the rest of her life. And so a woman whose marriage has lasted only a short time may find herself without any maintenance. Recently, one judge thought that 10p a month was the right order for a woman without children who had been deserted weeks after her marriage; he took the view that she was well able to work and fend for herself.

Loss of Pension Rights

A wife may often be worried that a divorce will affect her pension rights. The court may take this into account when deciding the amount of maintenance. Another factor the court may take into account is the conduct of the parties, but only when that conduct is really bad. Normally the judge will pay more attention to the length of the marriage and will tend to ignore the fact, say, that the wife has committed adultery.

Remarriage

Once the wife remarries, this cancels her right to be maintained by her former husband. Also if she goes to live with another man, the Court of Appeal has ruled the husband could apply for a reduction in his maintenance payments. Nevertheless, the former husband would always have to maintain his children.

Maintenance payments can be increased when the husband's means improve, say his salary rises. Similarly, the wife may ask for more if *her* expenses rise, eg her rent goes up. On the other hand, if her husband's salary goes down, he might be entitled to seek a reduction in payments.

Secured Periodical Payments

A husband who is wealthy and owns substantial assets, may find that the court will tie his periodical payments to the income from those assets. One advantage for his ex-wife of having her periodical payments secured to a particular asset is that his death would not affect her payments.

Share in the Family Assets

In addition to maintenance, the wife can expect from about one-third to one-half of the total family assets. The precise amount will vary according to all their circumstances including how long their marriage lasted as well as her 'contribution to the welfare of the family'.

Lump-Sum Payments

Sometimes it may be to the wife's advantage to take a lump sum in lieu of maintenance. This would especially apply if she planned to marry again, since on remarriage her right to maintenance would end. Similarly, if she wanted to buy a house or start a business a lump sum would be more useful. From her husband's point of view, paying a lump sum could have the effect of freeing him financially for the future. Even so, it should be pointed out, the court could still make a periodical payments order.

The Family Home

Very often the chief family asset is the home, which is usually in the husband's name. Even so, this does not necessarily mean that he can keep it in the event of a divorce. The judge has the power to order him to transfer it to his wife so that she and the children will have somewhere to live.

On the other hand, if the family home is the husband's sole financial asset, the court will not normally deprive him completely of his interest in it. In one case the husband owned their home jointly with his wife. The Court of Appeal allowed him to keep his half share in the home, although his wife and daughter were still living there, and ordered that the home should not be sold until the daughter had reached the age of seventeen.

Where the husband's behaviour has driven his wife out of the family home, the judge could turn the tables on him by ordering the husband out and the wife back in. But if the judge thought that the wife was *seriously and solely* to blame for the breakdown of their marriage (if her conduct was 'obvious and gross'), this could affect her rights, and might result in her receiving a smaller financial allowance, or even none at all.

4 Children

This chapter explains the ways in which the legal status of children differs from that of adults. It also sets out the rights and responsibilities of parents and tells you what is involved in adopting a child. For details of what may happen to the children when a couple separate, you should turn to the chapter on Marriage and Divorce. In this chapter, a 'child' means a person under eighteen, unless otherwise stated.

The Special Legal Status of Children

Contracts by Children

Children are not legally bound by most contracts which they make. However, this protection is not complete and if you are thinking of making a contract with a child or if you are yourself under eighteen you should consider to which of the following two classes it belongs:

1 The law regards some kinds of contract as being always against a child's interests and therefore they have been declared void by statute. The most important class of contracts to fall within this category are probably agreements for a loan. So no child can be bound by mortgage, which of course means that no child can obtain one. Most contracts to supply goods (and services) to a child are also void, unless they are for the necessities of life. Performance of these contracts cannot be enforced either by the child or by the other party and the child cannot be sued on them at all.

Nonetheless, if the contract has actually been carried out by both sides the child cannot get his money back. This is so even if the child had a bad bargain, unless he received absolutely no benefit at all. If you find that you have been caught by this rule, for instance by supplying goods for which the child then refuses to pay, it is no use for you to persuade him to confirm the contract after his eighteenth birthday. Even if you give him some additional benefit in return, confirmation is still of no legal effect.

2 Some contracts will usually be binding on a child: either contracts for 'necessaries' or service or apprenticeship contracts. Necessaries can include not only basic requirements such as food and clothing, but items which are needed to maintain the standard of living of the particular child. So one child's necessaries may be another child's luxuries. Even if you honestly believe that you are supplying a child with necessaries you will still be unable to demand payment if you turn out to be wrong.

Any agreement in the nature of a contract of apprenticeship (such as articles to a solicitor) is likely to be valid, because it will be regarded as being beneficial to the child—so if the child breaks the contract he might be liable for damages to his employer. However, as with all other contracts of personal service, the child cannot be forced to continue working against his will.

A child is not allowed to take unfair advantage of his privileges by inducing someone to make a contract with him on the pretence that he is an adult and then refusing to honour it. He may be compelled to give back what he has obtained in this way. (On the other hand, you are not entitled to assume that the person with whom you are dealing is an adult, unless he tells you that he is.)

Children's Civil Responsibility for their Acts

Except where a contract is involved, the civil courts will generally regard a child as liable for the consequences of his acts, unless he is obviously too young to be able to appreciate them. Consequently, children can be sued for such misdeeds as trespassing or wrongfully withholding goods. In practice, however, there will often be no point in suing a child for damages as he will have no money.

Despite this principle, children are still at an advantage when a case turns on a question of negligence. Legally, you owe your neighbour a 'duty of care' and if you fail to observe this you can be sued for negligence. The duty of care which you owe to a child is much higher than that which is owed to an adult and you will be liable accordingly.

Similarly, a child is much less likely than an adult to have damages which he is claiming refused or reduced on the ground that he was partly to blame for an accident. This will happen only if he failed to show the degree of care which could reasonably be expected from a child of his age.

Children's Rights over their Property

Children cannot hold the legal title to land, either freehold or leasehold. If you attempt to convey land to a child, the title stays with you but you become a trustee for him, which means you have to look after the property for him and hand it over to him when he comes of age. Similarly, when property (whether land, money or anything else) is left to a child under a will it will usually be held for him by trustees.

Apart from this, however, a child is in principle free to acquire and hold property in the same way as an adult (sometimes with the additional right to return any property which may prove a burden, because of liabilities attached to it). For instance, children can hold shares in a company, although the articles of some companies forbid this.

A child is also free in principle to dispose of his property, except when to do so would clearly be against his interest. However, he will sometimes have the power to get his property back again.

No one under eighteen can make a valid will (unless he is on active service in the armed forces).

Children as Civil Litigants

Generally, a child cannot start court proceedings himself, although he can bring an action in a county court for loss of earnings of up to £1,000. Therefore, if you think that your child has grounds for starting an action, you or some other suitable person must do so on his behalf. Unless you have any interest contrary to the child's, the court will allow you to do this without any formal order being made. You will be known as the child's 'next friend' and as such will be an officer of the court, responsible for the conduct of the child's case. You will be liable for the child's costs as if you were yourself the plaintiff. However, provided you acted properly in bringing the action, you will be permitted to recover them from the child, if he has any assets of his own.

In the same way, if your child is a defendant in a case, you or some other proper person will have to be appointed his 'guardian ad litem' and to conduct his case for him. Here again, the court will accept any reasonable guardian, although it may appoint one itself if need be. Whatever the outcome of a case, a child defendant will not usually be ordered to pay any costs.

The powers of next friends and guardians ad litem are limited.

If there are any proposals for a compromise settlement of an action in which a child is involved, the court's approval must be obtained before any agreement is reached. For instance, if a child is claiming damages for an injury and the defendant offers a sum of money in settlement, the sanction of the court must be sought before the offer is accepted. Similarly, the court must be asked to agree to any family arrangement which might affect the rights of children, for instance under a will trust.

Children and the Criminal Law

The law's attitude to children who commit criminal offences is basically a protective one. This is shown in the following ways:

1 No child under the age of 10 can commit a crime. Children aged 10–13 (inclusive) can be prosecuted, but it must be shown that they appreciated the difference between right and wrong.

Over the next few years prosecutions against children under 14 will be phased out (except in murder cases) and prosecutions against children aged 14–16 will become rare. But once a child is 17, he is for most purposes an adult in the eyes of the criminal law.

2 Charges against children are usually tried in private before magistrates in special Juvenile Courts. The exceptions to this are:

(i) If the child is 14–16 years old and is charged with a serious offence which could make him liable to a long sentence of detention, he will be tried by jury at the crown court.

(ii) If a child of 14 or over is charged jointly with an adult, he will stand trial with him in the adult court (whether a magistrates' court or a crown court).

Even in these exceptional cases, if the child is found guilty, he may still be remitted to the juvenile court which will decide how to treat him.

3 When a child is convicted, the juvenile court can deal with him in one of several ways, some of which would not be available in the case of an adult offender:

(i) The court may impose a fine.

(ii) The court may grant a discharge, either absolute or conditional on future good behaviour.

(iii) The court may order him to report to an attendance centre for a few hours every week.

(iv) For more serious offences or where there are several convictions, the child may be sent for a period to a detention centre.

(v) If the court feels that the child may get into more trouble, or if problems have arisen because of difficulties at home or for other reasons, it can make a supervision order. A supervisor will be appointed from the social services department of the local authority, who has to be the child's counsellor and friend and to assist the family if problems arise with the child. He will be in constant touch with the child who will, however, usually continue to live at home.

(vi) The court may make a care order, committing the child to the care of the local authority. In this case the authority will decide where the child is to live. It may leave him at home but it may consider the child needs the assistance of a residential school or a community home. Even if the child is left at home important decisions about his upbringing will have to be referred to the local authority. (For example, a decision may have to be taken on whether the child should receive remedial teaching.)

Court Orders can also be made where no specific offence has been committed. Any local authority may bring a child before a juvenile court if it reasonably believes that any of the following conditions apply:

(i) That his proper development is being avoidably prevented or neglected or his health is being avoidably impaired or neglected or he is being ill-treated; or

(ii) That it is possible that the condition set out in the proceeding paragraph applies, having regard to the fact that the court (or another court) has found that that condition applies (or did apply) to another child or young person who is (or was) a member of the same household; or

(iii) That he is exposed to moral danger; or

(iv) That he is beyond the control of his parent or guardian; or

(v) That he is of compulsory school age and is not receiving efficient full-time education suitable to his age, ability and aptitude; or

(vi) That he is guilty of an offence, excluding homicide.

If the court thinks that any of these conditions are satisfied and also that the child is in need of care or control which he is unlikely to receive, then it may make one of a number of orders, including a care order or a supervision order.

Finally, a local authority has a duty to receive into care any child in its area who has no parent or guardian, or who has been abandoned, or whose parents are for the time being unable to look after him. In such cases, the parents can ask for the child to be returned to them.

In addition the local authority also has power to assume full parental rights itself on any of the following grounds:

(i) That the parents are dead and that the child has no guardian; or

(ii) That a parent or guardian has abandoned him or suffers from some permanent disability rendering him incapable of caring for the child, or is of such habits or mode of life as to be unfit to have the care of the child.

If the parents dispute this, they can apply to the court, which will decide what is best for the child. If the court makes a care order in favour of the local authority, the parents can apply at a later date to have it revoked.

Children as Employees

In order to protect children against the kind of notorious exploitation which they suffered in the past, the law lays down extremely stringent rules about their employment.

1 Generally, no child under the age of 13 may be employed at all. Sometimes this is permitted in special circumstances. For instance, the employment of children under that age to appear on the stage or on television may be allowed, subject to suitable safeguards. Permission is not always needed, as when the performance is a very brief one or is arranged by the child's school.

2 Children of 13 and over who are still of compulsory school age, ie under 16, cannot be employed during usual school hours. There are strict limits on the times they can work outside school hours, including weekends. There is a general prohibition against employing children in this age group for heavy physical or industrial work.

3 No child under 18 may be employed for more than a certain number of hours. There are different limits for different occupations.

The Rights and Duties of Parents

A Parent's Rights

Parents have a general right to custody and control of their children. The degree of control lessens as the child grows older, and parents may lose control altogether even before the child reaches 18, if he or she marries or leaves home and becomes financially independent. Subject to this, a parent's principal rights are as follows:

1 Parents may restrict the liberty of their children in a reasonable way. For example, a father is entitled to keep his 14-year-old daughter indoors if he does not approve of the boyfriend who wishes to take her out. Traditionally, a parent's right physically to restrain a child against his or her will ended when his son reached 14 and his daughter reached 16. The modern courts might still regard this rule as a guide.

2 Parents may inflict corporal punishment on their children but this must be reasonable. Excessive punishment could leave a parent open to a charge of assault (and could have other consequences).

3 Parents have the theoretical right to require any child living at home to help with the domestic running of the house (even if the child is over 18). There is no legal way in which a parent can enforce this right and its only importance is that it does sometimes enable a parent to claim damages for a notional 'loss of services' when, for instance, a child has been injured through someone's negligence.

4 Although the minimum age of marriage is 16, the consent of the parent of a child under 18 is required. If this is refused, the child must apply to the court (usually, the magistrates' court) for consent instead. There is no appeal against the decision of the court. If the child manages to marry without any consent, the marriage will be valid. However, if the child had been made a ward of court, both parties to the marriage will be 'in contempt of court' and liable to penalties.

The attitude of the law is that parents should be able to control their children by themselves. If parents find that they have lost command, the law can help them only if they take the drastic step of bringing the child before the magistrates' court as being in need of care and control. Alternatively, they can apply to the High Court to make the child a ward of court (they will have to do the latter if they wish to prevent their child from marrying). Either course will probably result in the parent losing most of his say in the upbringing of the child, at least for a while.

A Parent's Responsibilities

1 Generally, parents are responsible for the physical care of their children and if they neglect or ill-treat them may be prosecuted for a criminal offence, and may lose custody.

2 There is a specific obligation on each parent to ensure that every child aged 5–16 receives efficient, full-time education suitable to his age and ability. This does not necessarily mean that parents have to send their children to school, provided they can educate them reasonably well at home.

If a parent fails in this duty, the local education authority can serve a school attendance order, requiring him to send his child to a specified school. Refusal to comply with the order is a criminal offence, although where practicable the parent may select another school.

Occasionally, parents keep their children at home because they are worried about the journey to school. It is permissible to do this on the grounds that the school is too far away (which means over two miles for a child under 8 and over three miles for an older child), unless there is a school bus. However, it is not a recognised objection that the route is too dangerous. As an example, the father of a school child contended that although the direct route from his home to school was within the maximum distance, his child had to go over a dangerous crossing; to avoid the crossing, he would have to take a longer route which was outside the statutory limit. The court held that this was no excuse as the distance was always measured by the shortest possible route and that the father was guilty of defying a school attendance order.

Parents are not allowed to keep their children away from school because they object to particular aspects of the school's curriculum. Furthermore, parents will usually not be fulfilling their duty to ensure their child's attendance if they persist in sending him to school when his appearance breaches school rules about, for instance, uniform or length of hair.

Parents' Liability for their Children's Acts

Any fine imposed on a child under 14 found guilty of a criminal offence will always be payable by the parent. If the child is between 14 and 16, the court has the option of ordering the parent to pay.

There is no general principle that a parent is responsible in the courts for the actions of his child. However, a parent or anyone in charge of a child may be liable if he negligently permits the child to use something dangerous or if he does not keep proper control over the child. This will apply even to things the child does that are quite normal for someone of his age if the parent should have foreseen the consequences.

Persons 'In Loco Parentis'

Guardians

Each parent has the right to appoint a guardian to assume parental control over his child. A guardian can be appointed by a formal deed during the parent's life, but the appointment is usually made by will. It will usually be expressed to take effect only if the other parent also dies while the child is under 18. However, a guardian may be appointed to act jointly with the surviving parent. If there is a dispute between them, the court can resolve it.

Guardians may also be appointed by the court, for instance, on the application of a surviving parent for someone to help him or her in the upbringing of the child, or on the application of any person who considers that the parent should not have sole custody.

For most purposes, the relationship between guardian and ward is the same as that between parent and child. However, the court will look with particular suspicion on any financial transactions between them, even if they occur some while after the ward reaches 18 and the guardianship ends. Unless the guardian can show that any dealings were fair to the child, they may be set aside. The guardian is also under a strict duty to look after any property of the ward which he has under his control.

Teachers

Parents are presumed to have delegated their rights to the teachers at their child's school. Consequently, teachers have the same rights of control over their pupils as parents have over their children, including the right to inflict reasonable punishment, such as caning or detention. A teacher's authority is not always confined solely to the child's behaviour during school hours.

Foster Parents and Child-minders

Generally, anyone who has custody of a child has most of the responsibilities of a parent for so long as it is in his charge. This applies to a local authority which has taken a child into care. However, in the case of individual foster parents who are not relatives or guardians, the upbringing of the child will be subject to the supervision of the local authority.

Similarly, persons running private nurseries for pre-school-age children are obliged to register with the local authority, unless they are doing it free of charge.

Disputes between Parents

Traditionally, a father had the sole right to custody of his child and to determine his education and religion. However, as the law now regards the mother, for most purposes, as the equal head of the family, disputes over such matters (in a marriage which is not breaking up) can, in theory, lead to an impasse which only the court can resolve.

If such disputes are taken to court, the chief consideration will be the welfare of the child. Thus if the dispute is over religion, and if the child already has fixed beliefs of his own, the court will be most reluctant to change them. In such cases, the court will, even today, probably prefer a child to have some religious upbringing rather than an agnostic or atheistic one, but will not prefer any one religion or denomination to another. However, the court may decide against a particular religious indoctrination if it thinks it will be contrary to the child's interests.

Unmarried Parents

In most cases an unmarried mother will have all the rights over her child which parents of a legitimate child have over theirs. The child's father does not have these rights, unless he has been given custody of the child by the court.

In any dispute over custody, whether with the child's father or with any other person or authority, the welfare of the child will be the paramount consideration. The fathers of illegitimate children have perhaps more often sought to avoid responsibility than to assume it. When this is so, the mother can apply to the magistrates' court to obtain financial support from the father. She must do this within three years of the child's birth, unless the father had been making payments and then stopped. A married woman who has a child by another man cannot bring affiliation proceedings unless she is not living with her husband and no longer has a right to be maintained by him.

The only provision which a father can be forced to make under an affiliation order is a weekly maintenance payment. The order automatically lapses when the father dies or when the child is adopted. (An adoption by the mother when she is still single will not have this effect even if she subsequently marries.)

If payments fall into arrears, the father will be brought before the court. The magistrates may then order him to pay off the arrears in instalments, or may remit some or all of them. Payments may be enforced by an 'attachment order', which obliges the father's employer to deduct them from his wages and to pay them to the court. As a last resort, the court can send the father to prison for failure to pay.

Adoption

When a child is adopted it becomes in the eyes of the law the child of the adopter, and ceases for all purposes to be the child of its natural parents. It will assume the surname of its adoptive parents, who may indeed also change its forenames. Again, the child will be as entitled as the other children of the family to a share in the estates of the adoptive parents on their deaths. At the same time, it loses all equivalent rights in the estates of its natural parents.

If you are thinking of adopting a child, you can make enquiries with the Association of British Adoption Societies, who will put you in contact with one of their member societies. These are all charities and are subject to state supervision.

To be eligible as adoptive parents a married couple must both be over 21, as must a single person. The parent of an illegitimate child will not be allowed to adopt the child alone unless the other parent is dead or cannot be found or there is some other reason justifying his or her exclusion.

The consent of the child's parents or guardians has to be obtained unless this is impossible or the consent is dispensed with (on the grounds, for instance, that they have neglected or ill-treated the child).

The child must live with the prospective adopters, or one of them, for at least a year before the adoption order. However, if the applicant, or one of the applicants, is a parent, step-parent or relative of the child, or if the child was placed with the applicants by an adoption agency or under a High Court order, the period is reduced to thirteen weeks. The court will want to satisfy itself that the adoption agency or local authority, as the case may be, has had sufficient opportunities to see the child in the applicants' home environment.

An application can be made to the High Court, the county court or the juvenile court. The procedure is similar in all cases but one advantage of the High Court, in cases where the adoptive parents want to maintain their anonymity, is that there may be a better chance of preserving secrecy than in a local court.

However, even in the county and juvenile courts, great pains are taken (where necessary) to prevent the natural and adoptive parents learning one another's identities. Proceedings are invariably held in private.

The court will investigate the applicants very thoroughly, aided by the child's 'guardian *ad litem*' whom it will appoint to protect the child's interests, and the 'reporting officer', who will usually be the same person. He will interview all relevant parties and will report back to the court.

Sometimes, the court will not come to a final decision and will make an interim order, allowing the couple to keep the child for a stated period of up to two years. After that, it may make a final order.

In some circumstances, the court may, instead of making an adoption order make a custodianship order.

Custodianship Orders

When the relevant provisions of the Children Act, 1975, come into force, certain people can apply to the court to be made the 'custodian' of a child. As the word implies, a custodian has 'legal custody' of the child, which means as much of a parent's legal right and duties as relates to the person of a child, including the place and manner in which his time is spent.

A custodianship order, although far-reaching, is thus more limited in scope than an adoption order. It does not, for example, affect the child's rights to his natural parents' and relatives' estates, or give him automatically any rights in the custodian's. Moreover, a custodian cannot arrange for the child to emigrate from the United Kingdom.

Those qualified to apply for a custodianship order are:

1 Any relative or (subject to some restrictions) step-parent of the child, if he or she applies with the consent of the person who then has legal custody and if the child has been living with him or her for three months before the application.

2 Any person with similar consent with whom the child has been living for periods totalling at least twelve months, including the three months before the application.

3 Any person with whom the child has been living for periods

totalling at least three years, including the three months before the application.

The parent of the child cannot apply.

The court may grant the order subject to certain conditions, for instance relating to rights of access for the parents.

The court can revoke the order on the application of the custodian or a parent or guardian or a local authority. It may then make such further orders as it may consider to be necessary for the care of the child.

Abortion

The law has always protected the rights of unborn children and it is still a criminal offence to procure an abortion. Both the mother and anyone helping her can be prosecuted. However, abortions are now legal if carried out by a doctor and for one of the following reasons:

1 That the continuance of the pregnancy would be a greater risk to the mother's life or to her physical or mental health than would its termination.

2 That the continuance of the pregnancy would involve a greater risk to the mother's other children than if it were terminated.

3 That there is a substantial risk of the child suffering from mental or physical abnormalities which would handicap it seriously.

Except in cases of genuine emergency, it is necessary for two doctors to certify that one of these conditions is fulfilled and for the abortion to be performed in an approved hospital or clinic.

If the mother is married, the consent of her husband is not required. Likewise, if she is 16 or over, her parents' consent is not needed. If a girl is under 16, her parents have to be consulted but even if they (or the girl herself) are against the abortion, it will then be legal if the doctors consider it necessary for the mother's health.

5 Wills and Probate

Making a Will

Making a will is not essential, provided the person is content that his assets should pass to his next of kin in the rigid order of priority laid down by the law (see p 61). But it is generally advisable for a number of reasons. In the first place, it makes matters more certain for the family of the deceased. Anyone who fails to make a will leaves his affairs in a state of uncertainty because there must always be the possibility that one day a will may be found and that it may contain provisions that no one had been able to allow for, for example, the deceased may have left his possessions to a charity and not to his family at all.

Where the relatives know that the deceased made a will but cannot find it after his death, there is a legal presumption that he cancelled it.

Advantages of a Will

The principal advantages of a will are that it allows the testator to:

Make a specific provision for each member of his family or other beneficiaries.

Appoint a guardian for minor children (under 18).

Declare whether he wishes to be buried or cremated (although this is not legally binding).

Leave his body to a medical school for anatomical purposes (although relatives can disallow this if they object).

Legal Requirements

Any person over 18 is entitled to make a will. Although the will does not have to follow any special form of wording, it is advisable to have it drawn up by a solicitor. A mistake in a will cannot be corrected once the person who made it has died. After death it becomes final and anything in it which is doubtful or ambiguous would have to be settled by the court in the event of a dispute.

The advantages of using a solicitor are that he will ensure that an acceptable wording is used; he will also be able to give skilled advice on such matters as capital transfer tax. In addition, he will have the will clearly typed and will keep a copy on file. Should the original then be accidentally destroyed or lost, the copy could be legally effective.

Witnesses

The testator must sign before two witnesses at the foot or end of the script. Anything written below his signature, even though in his own handwriting, is not legally part of the will. If he is infirm, his hand may be guided and if he is unable to write, he can make his mark. Also, if he makes his will under an assumed name, this too counts as a valid signature.

Strictly, each witness should watch the testator sign and the testator should then watch both witnesses sign in turn. A statement to this effect should appear alongside the signature, otherwise there will be difficulty when the time comes to prove the will. In such cases the Probate Registry will require a sworn statement by one of the witnesses that it was properly signed and witnessed. It is usual, therefore, for each witness to write his address and occupation so that he may be contacted if necessary.

If he is so ill or incapacitated that he is physically unable to sign, the testator may instruct another person, eg his doctor, to write his name for him. Provided the doctor signs in his presence, it counts as the testator's own signature. The fact that he directed his doctor to sign on his behalf must be stated.

No person who has signed as a witness is permitted to receive any gift under the will. Nor may a witness's wife or husband receive any benefit.

Exceptional Wills

There is one exception to the rule that a will must be in writing and properly signed and witnessed. A member of the armed forces who is on active service (even if under 18) is entitled to make a will without formalities, eg in the form of a letter. During active service, a soldier might say to a friend: 'Please see that my wife gets everything if I do not come through.' Such a declaration, even though not in writing, could operate as a valid will.

Choosing the Executor(s)

Naturally, the testator should choose his executor(s) with great care. An obvious person for him to appoint is whoever stands to receive the greatest benefit under it, eg his wife. He will be wise also to appoint a younger person, perhaps a son or daughter, to act as co-executor.

If the testator wishes to appoint someone other than a close relative, he should consult that person beforehand to make sure that he is agreeable. The duties of an executor can be time-consuming and, furthermore, an executor cannot ask to be paid for his trouble unless the will specifically allows it. Otherwise, he may claim only expenses such as travel, but nothing for his efforts or loss of time.

However, the executor may employ a solicitor to do all the legal paperwork involved in proving the will and winding up the estate, and in that case the latter's fees will count as an expense in the same way as funeral expenses do, and will be payable out of the assets of the deceased.

Professional Executors

Solicitors and accountants are often appointed as executors, especially if there are a large number of beneficiaries and legacies given under the will. In theory, solicitors' charges are based on the work involved in administering the estate, eg the number of letters written, time spent in interviews and on the telephone and time spent preparing documents. In practice solicitors and accountants tend to charge a percentage of the value of the assets involved. The percentage rate of charging is very much a rule-of-thumb method, because solicitors are entitled to increase their fees if the estate is unusually complex.

Banks, too, are sometimes appointed as executors. The chief advantage of appointing a bank is that by its nature as a large institution it offers a continuity which may be valuable if the will contains trusts which are likely to last many years. But it should be borne in mind that banks charge comparatively heavy fees, and are probably not to be recommended for the ordinary person's will.

When a Will Is Not Necessary

Gifts Made in Expectation of Death

A written will is not necessary in the case of a gift made by someone who expects shortly to die. For example, a mother on her deathbed may hand her daughter a box containing jewellery or the key to a safe or cupboard in which valuables are kept. The understanding in such a case would have to be that the daughter was to have the contents only if the mother died. If she recovered, her daughter would have to return the gift.

If the mother committed suicide, the gift would be invalid. Such gifts are legally effective only where death is anticipated from some natural or extraneous cause.

Nominations

Someone with his money in national savings or a friendly society can name on a special form the person he wishes to receive the money on his death. Although this type of nomination is not in the form of a will, it operates as a will. Thus, if the person nominated dies first, the nomination has no effect and, in the event of no other provision being made, the money would go to the owner's next of kin, not to the nominee's family.

Revoking or Changing a Will

Making a new will does not automatically cancel a previous will. To avoid confusion, the testator should always begin a new will by saying that he revokes all previous wills. However, if there is a contradiction, what is said in the later will prevails.

A testator can usually revoke his will by tearing it up or burning it, provided this is done intentionally and not by accident.

Cancellation by Marriage but Not by Divorce

Any will is automatically cancelled on marriage. If the testator should die without making a fresh will, his next of kin will inherit in the fixed order of priority (see p 61).

On the other hand, divorce does not revoke an existing will, which remains effective until a fresh one is made or the testator remarries.

It is important, therefore, to make a new will after a divorce as well as after a marriage.

Wills Made in Contemplation of Marriage

It is possible to make a will in advance of a marriage which will remain valid afterwards provided it refers specifically to the forthcoming marriage and mentions the name of the intended husband or wife.

Dying without a Will (Intestacy)

Where there is no will, or the will is declared invalid or not fully effective, a set of legal rules of inheritance then comes into operation.

Fixed Rules of Inheritance for a Married Person with Children

In the first place, the surviving husband or wife is entitled to all personal belongings. These do not have to be shared with the children or anyone else and include such items as the car, boat, household furniture and effects, jewellery, art or other collections (no matter how valuable), but not investments or items connected with business. For this reason, if a husband is for personal reasons reluctant to make a will, his wife may want to encourage him to invest in antiques, jewellery or other such objects which she can automatically inherit.

In addition to all personal belongings, the surviving wife or husband is also entitled to up to £15,000 in cash. The rest of the assets (if any) are divided into two equal portions. The income arising from one half goes to the widow or widower, as long as he or she lives. (Instead of income for life, he or she may opt to have an immediate cash sum of equivalent value.) On the death of the widow or widower the half share passes to the children. The other half of the deceased's assets is inherited by the children in equal shares. Each child is entitled to his or her share on reaching the age of 18, or sooner on marrying. If any child dies before becoming entitled, any children of his or hers will take their parent's share.

Married Persons with No Children

Where a person dies without leaving children, the wife or husband receives all personal belongings, plus £40,000 clear. The rest is divided into two equal portions. One half goes to the surviving husband or wife (in addition to the £40,000). The other half goes to the parents of the deceased, but if both parents are dead, then the remaining half will be shared by the deceased's brothers and sisters.

If there are no parents or brothers or sisters, and no nephews or nieces, the surviving husband or wife is entitled to everything.

The Family Home

Where there is no will the wife has an option to buy the family home at valuation in lieu of taking her share in cash.

No Surviving Wife or Husband

Where someone dies leaving no wife or husband, the next of kin, in the absence of a will, will inherit in the following order:

1 The children share everything equally. If one child is already dead, his or her share will go automatically to his or her children, ie the grandchildren.

2 If someone dies leaving no spouse or children (and no grandchildren), the parents of the deceased inherit everything.

3 The brothers and sisters share the estate if both parents are already dead. Where any of these have already died their share goes to their children, the nephews and nieces of the deceased.

4 Where there are no full brothers or sisters, the half-brothers and half-sisters can inherit.

5 Next in order of priority come the grandparents. They are followed by the uncles and aunts, or their children if the uncles or aunts have already died.

Moral Claims

Where no member of the above classes of relative is alive, the Crown inherits everything. But usually the Crown will observe any moral claim to the estate. For example, if the deceased had written a letter leaving everything to a close friend, the Crown would usually honour such a claim even though it was not based on a valid will.

Illegitimate and Adopted Children

Nowadays illegitimate children can inherit the property of their deceased parent. Also, adopted children now count as the children of their adopted parents for purposes of inheritance.

When Children May Inherit

Normally, no child can receive his share until he reaches his eighteenth birthday. But if, with the consent of his guardians, he marries sooner, he is entitled to have his share on marriage.

Proving a Will—The Probate Registry

When a person dies, his will must be presented for probate. Probate is the legal process by which the court accepts the will as valid and gives the executor a document which authenticates his legal powers.

Most executors leave this to their solicitors, but in recent years it has been found that approximately one in seven proves the will himself. Although it is a complex and time-consuming business, the amount of money saved could make the effort worthwhile, especially in the case of the smaller estate. The Probate Registry recognises this and in fact has a special department called the Personal Application Department.

The principal probate registry is now called the Principal Registry of the Family Division of the High Court. Outside London there are local probate registries whose addresses can be found in the telephone directory.

'Do-It-Yourself' Probate

'Do-It-Yourself' executors are charged an additional fee because of the extra work done by the staff at the registry, but the eventual saving to the executor more than justifies this added expense. In some cases, however, particularly if the estate is large and land or buildings are involved, a solicitor might be needed at some stage.

Proving a will may be divided into seven principal stages:

1 The executor first draws up a list of all assets of the deceased, eg his house, furniture, savings, investments and personal belongings. Against each item should be marked its approximate value, which would be obtained if it was sold, say, at auction. In the case of personal belongings, this is not likely to be great, and the probate registry would accept a rough estimate.

As to the value of a house, inquiries of local estate agents would give an indication of the value of similar properties. If the house is owned jointly by the deceased and his wife, then only half its value should be listed. The value of stocks and shares can be ascertained by referring to prices quoted in the daily press, or by approaching the companies concerned, and so on.

2 Next the executor prepares a list of all the debts of the deceased, including the funeral expenses.

3 He then takes these two lists together with the will and death certificate to the local probate registry and asks for the personal application department. (It would also be wise to take along all deposit account books and share and savings certificates.)

4 At the registry, the executor will be given a form on which to enter details of death and the next of kin. He will also be given another form on which to write details of the assets and debts already listed. House property is listed on a separate form and details of company shares held by the deceased on another form.

5 A second visit must then be made to the registry after it has had time to check the forms and prepare the official documents for signature by the executor. These are:

The executor's oath, in which he promises to deal with the assets of the deceased in accordance with the terms of his will.

The capital transfer tax form.

6 At this stage, two cheques must be handed to the registry officials. These cover:

A further fee based on the value of the assets of the deceased.

A cheque in payment of any capital transfer tax required (see also p 67).

7 A month or so later the probate registry will send the document of probate to the executor with a photocopy of the will attached to it. The registry will keep the original will. The executor can then send an official photocopy of the probate to the bank, or anyone else who holds assets of the deceased, as proof that the executor is entitled to have those assets transferred to him. He can then allot them as the will directs.

Who May Benefit under a Will

Only a person who outlives the testator can inherit a gift under his will. If the beneficiary is already dead, the gift to him fails. For example, a man may leave his car to a friend. But if the friend dies first, the car forms part of the testator's general (or 'residuary') estate.

Exception in Favour of Children or Grandchildren

There is one important exception to the above rule. This applies where the testator leaves something to one of his own children or grandchildren by name. It will not then matter if the person named dies first. In that case, the legacy will be regarded as part of the assets of the person named, and will go to whoever is entitled under his or her will.

Persons Causing the Death of the Testator

Anyone who is guilty of murder or manslaughter cannot take any benefit under the will of the person killed. This rule does not apply where the killer was insane. But if he is guilty of manslaughter by reason of diminished responsibility, he cannot benefit under the will of the victim. However, where the victim makes his will in the interval between his injuries and his death, the gift will stand. It will also do so if he reaffirms an earlier will in favour of the guilty person before he succumbs to his injuries.

When a Legacy May Be Disallowed

The law assumes that a properly signed will is valid unless there are suspicious circumstances, eg where the person who prepared the will receives a large benefit. It is then up to that beneficiary to prove that the deceased was fully aware of, and approved, the contents of his will and that he signed it without any persuasion.

Contesting a Will

The relatives opposing the will may be able to show that a particular beneficiary used some form of coercion. If they can show that he put pressure on the testator and so forced him to make a will that he did not really want to make, the court will declare the will void and allow the testator's next of kin to inherit his assets.

It may be that the person who persuaded the deceased to make him a particular gift had a confidential relationship with him, eg as his religious, medical, legal or financial adviser. In such cases the law presumes undue influence was used, and the beneficiary forfeits the gift.

Inheritance (Family Provision Act)

Persons other than those who benefit under a will or under intestacy may be able to claim against the estate under the Inheritance (Provision for Family and Dependants) Act, 1975. The following persons may claim under the Act:

(a) the wife or husband of the deceased;

(b) a former wife or former husband of the deceased who has not remarried;

(c) a child of the deceased;

(d) any person (not being a child of the deceased) who, in the case of any marriage to which the deceased was at any time a party, was treated by the deceased as a child of the family in relation to that marriage;

(e) any person (who is not included in any of the above categories) who immediately before the death of the deceased was being maintained, either wholly or partly, by the deceased.

If the court is satisfied that the will or intestacy did not make reasonable provision for the claimant, it may order provision for the claimant to be made out of the estate, either by periodical payments or by a lump sum or both. If the claimant is the deceased's widow or widower, the court may make such provision as it thinks reasonable. Otherwise, it may make only such provision as is required for the claimant's maintenance. If the deceased gave away any property within six years of his death and if the court is satisfied that the gift was made with the intention of defeating an application for financial provision under the Act, the recipient of the gift may be ordered to make financial provision for the claimant. Similarly, if the deceased was the co-owner of any property and on his death his part share passed to the other co-owner or co-owners, provision may be ordered out of that share.

Claims should be brought within six months of the executors obtaining probate of the will (or, where no executors have been appointed within six months, of the administrators obtaining letters of administration). The court may permit late applications.

Capital Transfer Tax

Capital transfer tax is payable by a person's executor or administrator when he dies. Generally, it is assessed on the value of the estate at the date of death. A table of the rates is shown in the table below. It will be noted from this that no tax is payable on estates worth less than £15,000. Subject to certain exemptions, gifts made by the deceased in his lifetime will be included in the value of his estate for tax purposes if they were made either after 26 March 1974 or before that date but within seven years of his death. If the total of taxable gifts during his lifetime exceeds £15,000, tax will be paid when gifts are made after this total has been exceeded. However, the rates of tax on such lifetime gifts are lower, unless these are made within three years of death.

No tax is payable on property which is transferred to a husband or wife, either by a lifetime gift, by a will or under the intestacy rules. However, if a husband leaves his estate to his wife (or vice versa), the whole of the joint assets will be taxed on the death of the widow or widower. This will mean more tax is paid overall as the combined estate will attract a higher rate of tax. If husband and wife each have substantial estates they can save tax by leaving at least some of their assets in favour of their children (or anyone else). For example, if a husband and wife each have estates of £30,000 and leave them all to each other, there will be no tax on the first death. However, if on the death of the survivor his or her estate is worth £60,000, the tax will be £11,250. If they each left their estates to their children, the tax would be £2,250 on each death, which would mean a total tax bill of £5,500.

It is possible for the provisions of a will or intestacy to be varied for tax purposes within two years of death by way of family agreement, provided certain conditions are fulfilled. Therefore, in the first of the above examples the widow could waive her right to the estate and thus achieve the overall tax saving.

The rules of capital transfer tax are very complex. Anyone wanting to save tax by his will or otherwise should consult his solicitor or other professional adviser.

Higher Scale of Rates of Capital Transfer Tax

Deaths on and after 13 March 1975

	Amount chargeable	*Rate per cent*	*Cumulative amount chargeable*	*Cumulative total tax*
1st	£15,000	—	£15,000	—
Next	£5,000	10	£20,000	£500
	£5,000	15	£25,000	£1,250
	£5,000	20	£30,000	£2,250
	£10,000	25	£40,000	£4,750
	£10,000	30	£50,000	£7,750
	£10,000	35	£60,000	£11,250
	£20,000	40	£80,000	£19,250
	£20,000	45	£100,000	£28,250
	£20,000	50	£120,000	£38,250
	£30,000	55	£150,000	£54,750
	£350,000	60	£500,000	£264,750
	£500,000	65	£1,000,000	£589,750
	£1,000,000	70	£2,000,000	£1,289,750
Any remainder		75		

These are the higher rates which are applicable to transfers on the death of the transferor or within three years before death.

6 Buying and Owning a Home

Ownership

Ownership of a house may be either freehold or leasehold. Houses are generally freehold, which means ownership is permanent. Flats and maisonettes are usually leasehold, which means there is a time limit on the duration of ownership.

Freehold	**Leasehold**
Freehold land is owned without any limitation of time.	The owner of a lease keeps it for a fixed number of years only. This may be a short lease, say for three years, or a monthly tenancy or it may be for as long as ninety-nine years or more.
The freeholder is absolute owner. In theory he holds directly from the Crown, free of any payment.	Leaseholder has to pay rent to landlord. In the case of a long lease this is called 'ground rent', which can vary from £20 to £400 a year or more. If the leaseholder does not pay the ground rent, the landlord can claim the property back.
The freeholder can treat his property as he likes and can let it fall into disrepair if he chooses.	The leaseholder is strictly bound by the terms of the lease and will generally have to keep the house in repair.
There may be restrictive covenants, eg which prevent	Usually the lease will forbid him using the house except as a private

Freehold	Leasehold
business use, or impose building restrictions. But no restrictive covenant can ever involve the freeholder in having to pay out money.	dwelling. If so, he may not use part of it as an office. Likely to be numerous other restrictions. If leaseholder breaks an important term of his lease, landlord can apply to the court to evict him. In this case he could lose the lease, and the money he paid for it.
Subject always to market conditions, a freehold house usually tends to hold or increase in value.	A leasehold house may tend to go down in value as the lease gets shorter. A ninety-nine-year lease will naturally sell for more than a lease with only twenty years left to run.
It is usually possible to get a loan on a freehold house from a building society.	It can be more difficult to obtain a mortgage advance to buy a leasehold house. If there are less than forty years left to run, some building societies will refuse to make a loan.

Converting Leasehold to Freehold

Many leaseholders now have the right to convert their lease into a freehold. Alternatively, they can ask for a fifty-year extension. Whether conversion is possible depends on the rateable value. The rating department of the local authority will be able to advise on this.

A leaseholder will be entitled to buy the freehold from his landlord, provided:

He has been living in his house for the last five years.

He lives in a house, not a flat or maisonette.

The original lease was more than twenty-one years long. (It does not matter that only two or three years may now remain.)

The leaseholder must not wait until his lease has come to an end. Otherwise he will lose his right to buy the freehold.

Cost of Freehold

It does not matter that part of the house is used as a shop or for business, so long as the leaseholder lives there. If a price cannot be agreed privately, the Lands Tribunal will fix a fair price.

Buying a New House

Guarantee of Quality

Every house-builder should be prepared to guarantee his product. This will be in addition to the guarantee automatically given by law which says that a building must be constructed in a good workmanlike manner.

The best guarantee of quality is a certificate from the National House-Builders Registration Council which will cover defects up to £20,000. The buyer should ask the builder if he belongs to this scheme and can issue a certificate of guarantee under it. If so, the buyer should inform his solicitor, who will ensure that the certificate of guarantee is included in his contract to buy the house.

Buying an Older House

Supposing you decide to buy an older house: how can you best protect your interests? The first rule to remember is that, basically, you take the house as you find it. Therefore, question the estate agent, or owner, or both, in detail about the state of drains, condition of the central heating, plumbing and so on. Although the seller of a second-hand house gives no guarantee, both he and the house agent must answer all questions truthfully.

The buyer may, for example, ask whether there is any wood rot or woodworm. If the seller or the agent tells him that there is none, and it later turns out that the woodwork is infested with dry rot, the seller would be liable under the Misrepresentation Act, 1967. He could escape liability only if he satisfies the judge:

1 He genuinely believed that there was no wood rot; and

2 He had good reason for thinking there was none.

From the buyer's point of view, it would be easier to obtain compensation if the seller or the agent stated in a letter that there was no wood rot. But such a statement does not have to be in writing, though in practice it would be easier to prove if someone else was present when he said it. This is one reason why a couple buying a house should inspect it and join in all discussions together.

The seller is also liable for any misrepresentation the estate agent may make in negotiating the sale, even though made innocently.

Is the House under Guarantee?

If the house is less than ten years old, the buyer should find out whether the original buyer obtained a certificate from the National House-Builders Registration Council (see also above). If so, he will get the benefit of it for the unexpired term.

Fixtures and Fittings

In law, a fixture or fitting which has become part of the structure of the property may not be removed on departure. This applies particularly to items built in to the walls, such as cupboards and kitchen units which are permanently attached to the structure. Similarly, any part of a central heating system or a plumbing system, such as bathroom appliances and the electrical wiring system, must be left intact.

Where there is a fixture or fitting which could be removed, the seller should be asked to confirm that he will be leaving it. This would apply, for example, to curtain appliances, fixed electric fires, fitted carpets, linoleum, etc. Sometimes wardrobes and cupboards can be easily removed although they appear to be built-in. It is up to the buyer to make sure that these are listed as included in the sale of the house, and that in due course his solicitor receives a copy of the list. Sometimes, by having the fixtures and fittings separately priced, the solicitor will be able to save his client some stamp duty (see also p 85).

Employing a Surveyor

In general, if a house is not covered by the original builder's guarantee (ie if more than ten years old) it is wise to employ a qualified surveyor to carry out a thorough overall examination of the house before contracts are exchanged, ie before you are legally obliged to buy the house (see also p 78). (Normally the surveyor will tell you in advance what his fee will be for this service.) A private surveyor will take special care that his report is accurate because he will be liable to pay compensation if it is not. For example, if he assures his client that the drains are sound, and they start to give trouble after the client has moved in, he will be responsible for paying the cost of putting them right.

Agreeing to Buy

After inspecting the house, and usually before commissioning a full survey, the would-be buyer will need to agree a price, either directly with the seller or through his estate agent. During these negotiations it is important to remember that:

Until the buyer has signed a document agreeing to buy, and has handed it to the seller, he may change his mind if for any reason he decides not to go ahead. Every buyer should take care not to sacrifice this right.

One danger is that a detailed letter written by the buyer agreeing the price during negotiations may be regarded in law as binding. Thus the buyer could find himself in the situation where he is bound to buy but where the seller—because he has not signed a similar letter—cannot be compelled to sell if he changes his mind. The same predicament could happen to the seller if he sends a full letter agreeing to the sale.

'Subject to Contract'

To avoid this, buyers and sellers alike should head any letter they may write about the house with the words 'subject to contract'. A prospective buyer should state that his offer is 'subject to contract and survey'. These words will operate to prevent him being legally bound by any offer he may make until his solicitors advise him that contracts are ready to be exchanged.

Both parties should remember, too, that any expense they incur, in survey or legal fees, will be lost if for any reason the buyer or seller decides to withdraw before exchange of contracts.

Deposits

The estate agent may ask the buyer for a sum of money as a deposit. He may ask for a full deposit, ie 10 per cent of the purchase price, or he may ask for a smaller sum, say £50, before he will accept the buyer as serious. In practice, it may be difficult for the buyer to avoid paying him a *nominal* deposit to show his genuine wish to buy but he should resist paying the agent the full 10 per cent of the price agreed for the house. Most reputable estate agents abide by the normal procedure whereby the buyer pays his deposit to the seller's solicitor when contracts are exchanged, and not before. All standard forms of contract stipulate for payment of a deposit of 10 per cent (but no more) of the price of the house.

The layman may in his innocence ask why it is necessary to pay a deposit at all. As usual, the lawyers have an answer. Once the seller signs and exchanges contracts with the buyer for sale of his house, the law gives the buyer an immediate interest in it called a 'lien'. Also, the seller becomes a trustee of the house for him. The buyer can register this lien and so block the sale of the house to anyone else. If he is to receive these rights, it is only fair he should pay a deposit. If he backs out of buying, he forfeits his deposit. The seller's solicitor is negligent if he fails to advise the seller to insist on a deposit being paid when contracts are exchanged.

Under the present law the seller who appoints a solicitor (or estate agent) to hold the 10 per cent deposit as stakeholder is usually disappointed to find that at the close of the transaction the stakeholder keeps the interest on it.

This appears to run counter to the ruling that solicitors are strictly accountable for interest on sums in excess of £500 if held for more than a few weeks. If in doubt, a client can ask the Law Society to certify how much interest he is entitled to. In the case of an expensive house or flat, interest can be a significant item if the deposit is held for a long period. Recently a High Court judge decided that estate agents too can keep the interest earned on a deposit, provided they declare on the receipt that they are 'stakeholders'.

Safeguarding the Deposit

Who is liable for a lost deposit? A dishonest estate agent may accept several deposits on the same house. If he defaults, say disappears or goes bankrupt, the vendor is not responsible to repay each prospective purchaser his pre-contract deposit. But once contracts have been exchanged with a particular purchaser the vendor will suffer its loss, if the contract authorises the estate agent to hold the deposit.

Both vendor and purchaser should insist that the deposit is paid over by the purchaser's solicitor to the vendor's solicitor when contracts are exchanged, in accordance with the usual practice.

Deposit to be Held as 'Stakeholder'

The contract should state that the vendor's solicitor will hold the deposit as 'stakeholder'. This means the vendor cannot receive it until the sale is finalised, ie after completion. Where a solicitor (or estate agent) receives a deposit 'as agent for the vendor', the vendor can have it at once to use as he wishes.

It is much safer for both buyer and seller to insist that all payments are made through or to their respective solicitors, each of whom is covered in the event of dishonesty by the Law Society's compensation fund.

Compensation for Lost Deposits

Compensation schemes to repay lost deposits are run by:

1 The Royal Institution of Chartered Surveyors.

2 The Society of Valuers and Auctioneers.

3 The National Association of Estate Agents.

The house-buyer who mourns his lost deposit must first report the defaulting estate agent to the police for fraud before he can make a claim. Not all estate agents belong to one of the above professional associations. Make sure you deal with one who does.

Estate Agents' Commission

When selling a house through an estate agent it is the seller who is liable to pay the agent commission for introducing the prospective buyer.

Most estate agents use a standard form of undertaking relating to commission which the seller is required to sign when giving them instructions to sell. It binds the seller to pay commission in the event of their finding 'a ready, able and willing' purchaser at the price stated or any other price the seller agrees to accept.

It could happen that the seller might become liable to pay commission, even though the sale falls through. For example, the seller may be asking £20,000 for his house. Smith & Co put forward a purchaser at £17,000. After some delay the seller may find that, owing to financial pressures, he has no alternative but to accept this lower offer, even though it involves him in considerable loss. Shortly after, another firm, Jones & Co, may come up with an offer at the original asking price of £20,000. If he accepts the higher offer, the seller will then be liable to pay commission both to Smith & Co and Jones & Co.

The best advice one can give to a seller who proposes to instruct more than one agent, is to make it clear to each that he will pay commission only on the completion of the purchase. This means that the seller will not have to pay commission until he has the whole of the proceeds of sale in his bank account, and only to the agent who introduced the successful purchaser.

Solicitors and Conveyancing

How to Choose a Solicitor

The document which transfers ownership from seller to buyer is a 'conveyance'; hence solicitors refer to house-buying transactions as 'conveyancing'. It is a complicated procedure which is best left to them.

Choose a firm of solicitors near your home, or ask your building society to recommend one who will also act for the society on the mortgage. This will save legal costs.

Do not attempt the legal work yourself, unless you have legal training.

Do not use a solicitor who is recommended by the estate agents; should a dispute occur, his loyalty could be to them rather than to you.

Do not use any person who is not a qualified solicitor, or any association which offers you 'cheap conveyancing'. They can be unreliable.

Buying a House outside England or Wales

Anyone who contemplates buying property abroad, or in Scotland or Northern Ireland, must employ a solicitor there, since the local land law is very different from English law. Such a buyer could, however, start by consulting an English solicitor who would then instruct local solicitors to act in his purchase. Although using English solicitors might be more expensive, in the long run it might be prudent especially if the buyer lives in England.

Advantages of Using a Solicitor

There are many ways in which a solicitor can be of help for there are legal technicalities and pitfalls in the conveyancing process. For example:

1 *Gazumping.* A buyer may be anxious to clinch his purchase for fear of being gazumped. Here it is the duty of his solicitor to warn the buyer of the dangers of signing a binding contract before he has obtained sufficient funds; this may well include the definite promise of a loan from a building society.

A solicitor who failed to make this clear to his client would be responsible for his client's financial loss if he exchanged contracts without receiving confirmation of the loan. If the buyer could not then find the full purchase money, and had to withdraw from his purchase, he would lose his deposit, ie 10 per cent of the purchase price. Moreover, he might have to pay a further sum by way of damages if the seller then had to find another buyer at a lower price. If this situation were to arise it would be the solicitor's duty to get the buyer out of his difficulties, or indemnify him against any loss.

2 *Information from Local Searches.* A solicitor will give technical advice on whether a house is in a town planning scheme, likely to be affected by new roads, or any other developments (see also below).

3 *Enquiries before Contract.* He will also obtain a great deal of important and useful information about the house from the seller who is required to answer a long questionnaire before exchange of contracts. Provided the replies given are satisfactory, the buyer's solicitor will then exchange contracts. If the buyer later finds he has been given the wrong information, he may be able to claim compensation under the Misrepresentation Act.

4 *Stamp Duty.* A solicitor may be able to save his client stamp duty by arranging for carpets and fittings, etc to be priced separately from the house itself.

Professional Guarantee

The solicitors' professional body—the Law Society—guarantees all clients against any loss if a solicitor defaults or becomes bankrupt. Should a member of a particular firm make off with a client's money, the client will be compensated in full. Should the buyer's solicitor make an error in law he will have to compensate the buyer for any loss. Solicitors have an insurance scheme to cover mistakes.

Exchange of Contracts

Exchange of contracts is the most important step in buying a house. By exchanging signed contracts, the buyer and seller bind themselves to go ahead with the transaction. Thereafter, the seller cannot offer the property to anyone else at a higher price, and the buyer cannot drop out if he sees another property he likes better. Their respective solicitors are the only persons who can advise when it is safe to exchange contracts. Once each has posted the signed part to his opposite number and received the other part in exchange, both buyer and seller are then legally bound.

The legal effect of exchanging contracts is that although the house still belongs in law to the seller he must henceforth hold it as trustee for the buyer. If it increases in value thereafter, the benefit will be the buyer's.

The buyer would stand to lose his deposit if, having signed a contract to buy, he failed to complete his purchase. Equally, the seller too could be made to pay damages if he refused to go ahead or could not fulfil the terms of his agreement. For example, if the buyer is not given full legal ownership and vacant possession, he can sue the seller for substantial compensation. (Just how much depends on the extent to which property values have risen in the meantime.)

Risk of Fire and Flood after Exchange of Contracts

After exchanging contracts the buyer must at once take out an insurance policy. If the house burns down he will have to bear the loss. This does not mean the seller can safely cancel his own policy of insurance. He will be foolish to let his policy expire until the whole purchase price is in his bank. Admittedly, if the house burns down, in law he can insist that the buyer still completes the purchase, ie pays the full price. In practice, if the buyer has not insured, he might go bankrupt and the seller would never get his money.

Leasehold flats must usually be insured with the insurance company nominated in the lease. In this case the buyer's solicitor will ask the seller of the flat to give an undertaking not to cancel the policy. The buyer must pay the premium from the date of exchange of contracts, but the seller will hold the policy in trust for the buyer's benefit until completion. So if, before completion, the flat is damaged by fire, the buyer will be entitled to claim on the policy.

Buying One House and Selling Another

It is vital that, as a buyer, you do not contract to buy a new house until you have sold your present house. The delicate operation of dovetailing both transactions is best left to the skill of your solicitor. He will arrange to exchange contracts on each, to sell one and buy the other simultaneously. This is one reason why house-buying is often so protracted an operation. But delay may be inevitable. Unless you are wealthy enough to be able to own both houses at once, you should not be tempted to exchange contracts on your new house—no matter how attractive it may be—until the buyer of your old one is similarly willing to exchange.

If you are changing jobs and must move home, your bank will usually grant you a bridging loan for the period when your old house is still unsold.

Before Contracts Can Be Exchanged

Before exchange of contracts the buyer's solicitor will make a variety of checks and inquiries about the house. He will ascertain whether the title deeds contain restrictions on the use of the house, eg prohibiting use for business purposes or against extending it or having sheds or caravans in the garden (see also p. 76). (Such restrictions are particularly likely if you are buying a leasehold house or flat.) He will also check with the local authority that their registers show nothing which affects the house. Some possible town planning snags are:

The house is shown as adjoining a road which is likely to be widened; this could mean losing part or all of an attractive garden.

There is a road to the rear of the house which is not made up or maintained by the local authority. If, at some future date, the local authority decided to make up the surface, it would charge a proportionate cost against the house—possibly several hundred pounds, depending on frontage.

The house is shown as situated in a redevelopment area; perhaps a large block of flats will be erected nearby.

The house is listed as being 'of special architectural interest'; this may mean that your proposed alterations are out of the question.

The house is scheduled for demolition under a redevelopment scheme due to take effect in, say, five or ten years.

Inspecting the House and Checking Boundary Lines

Generally, a solicitor will not inspect the house personally, but will leave this to the buyer and the buyer's surveyor. He will usually provide the buyer with a copy of the plan of the house, showing where the boundaries are. It is up to the buyer himself, or his surveyor, to check that the dimensions shown on the plan are correct and that the positions of fences and walls correspond with those around the house.

Checking and Transferring Legal Ownership

Before he can prepare a form of transfer of ownership or 'conveyance' the chief task of the buyer's solicitor is to check the documents which prove the seller's 'title' or ownership, ie to confirm that he has the legal right to sell. This is fairly straightforward where the seller is registered as owner at the Land Registry. If so, he will usually have an absolute title which is guaranteed by the state. Instead of examining numerous deeds, as is the case with unregistered conveyancing, the solicitor will have only one main document to check—the Land Registry certificate of title.

The system of registration of title to land is slowly spreading but there are still many areas where registration of title is not yet required. It is government policy eventually to extend registration of title to all land in the United Kingdom.

One of the advantages of registered title is that it is guaranteed by the state that the person in whose name the certificate of title is issued is in fact the rightful owner. The state therefore undertakes to pay compensation if such title proves to be false or faulty.

On each change of ownership the Land Registry charges a fee for transfer, which increases with the value of the property transferred. A buyer cannot avoid paying this fee to the Land Registry because if he fails to register his title will be valueless in law.

Unregistered Title

In country districts, ownership of houses is generally not recorded at the Land Registry, and it may be a complicated task for the solicitor to verify all the documents proving ownership. He will have to check the conveyances to previous purchasers to make sure that each is in order and that there is no link in the chain of ownership which is unsatisfactory. For example, where a previous owner died, the solicitor will verify that the personal representatives of the deceased were in fact his rightful personal representatives in law and so were entitled to convey the property to the next owner. Formerly the chain of title had to be checked back in this way for thirty years, but this has now been reduced to fifteen.

Importance of Searches

The buyer's solicitor will also seek to confirm by making a search at the land charges registry that the seller has not been made bankrupt and that there is nothing affecting ownership, such as an unpaid mortgage. He will advise against completing and paying over the purchase money until certain that the Land Charges Register is clear. To take another example, an official search might reveal that the seller's wife has registered herself under the Matrimonial Homes Act. This gives her a right to stay in the house. The result would be that no buyer could get her out.

Legal Protection for the Buyer

The passing of the Misrepresentation Act, 1967, has greatly strengthened the hand of the buyer who is given wrong information by the seller or estate agent. Prior to this act the law gave the buyer little protection, except on the following points:

1 That the seller was entitled to sell.

2 That no one should interfere with his 'quiet enjoyment' of the house.

3 That there were no liabilities on the house.

(Also, in the past, if the seller had been dishonest, the buyer was able to claim damages.)

Damages for Incorrect Information

Under present-day law, even if the seller innocently misleads him, the buyer may claim damages under the Misrepresentation Act, and may even insist on the seller taking the house back. This liability extends to all the information given to the buyer's solicitor in answer to a long questionnaire called 'enquiries before contract'.

Mistake in Buyer's Favour

If, by some error, the seller included in the contract a piece of land he did not intend to sell, eg part of a field adjoining a cottage, this would be to the buyer's advantage and would go with the cottage, provided it was shown on the plan as part of the property sold. Similarly, if the seller described the cottage and garden as measuring half an acre, when it turns out in fact to be two acres, the buyer would benefit from this error in his favour.

Insurance

The moment that contracts are exchanged, complete responsibility for the property falls on the buyer, even though he has not yet paid for it and it may be several months before he actually does so. In practice, a building society features in most purchases and it usually insists on arranging the insurance of the structure. The buyer's solicitor notifies the society to effect cover from the date contracts are to be exchanged. Similarly, anyone buying a long lease will usually find that the landlords insist on the house or flat being insured through the insurance company of their choice.

The buyer should also see that his furniture and household belongings are covered by insurance. He can ask the building society's insurers to let him have a proposal form or arrange it with an insurance company of his own choice. This policy may carry with it useful extensions at very little extra charge. For example, liability of the householder to visitors is desirable in case anyone should be injured while on his premises.

Completion of the Purchase

To complete the purchase the buyer's solicitor hands over the balance of the price agreed for the house, and receives in return the documents transferring ownership. Usually, the buyer is entitled to the keys and to full vacant possession. This procedure is called 'completion of the purchase' and usually takes place at the offices of the seller's solicitors. Payment is made by a banker's draft which, unlike a cheque, cannot be stopped.

Vacant Possession

If the seller promises full vacant possession, and there is still a tenant living in the house, the buyer could claim heavy damages.

Where the buyer knows that there have been tenants in the house, it is a wise precaution to go there a few days before the date fixed for completion to check that they have gone. If they are still there, he should instruct his solicitors to delay payment until the house is completely empty.

Ownership of the New House

When buying, a couple will be asked whether they wish to own their house in their joint names or in the husband's name alone or whether the wife is to be the sole owner. For the average family, co-ownership is preferable.

Co-ownership

There are two types of co-ownership—joint or in common. These are discussed more fully in Chapter 2 but, in brief, joint ownership is the best form of co-ownership for the average married couple. Its most important feature is that on the death of one of them, the survivor automatically acquires ownership of the whole property.

In practice, ownership in common is not usual for a married couple, unless they want to be strictly businesslike. For example, if the husband puts up £2,000 of the purchase money, and the wife £6,000, they could ask their solicitors to state on the transfer that their respective shares are one-quarter and three-quarters.

When a Trust Arises

Normally, once the house is bought it belongs to the person whose name appears on the land certificate, or conveyance. But if paid for either partly or wholly with money provided by another person, the result may be that the legal owner holds it in trust for the benefit of the person who put up the money. For example:

1 The house is bought with money belonging to the wife, but is transferred into the husband's name. He holds it as trustee for her benefit and he is obliged in law to deal with it exactly as she instructs him.

2 Similarly where part of the money is advanced by the wife the husband is obliged to pay his wife part of the proceeds if he sells it.

3 He also holds the house on trust if a relative, for example his wife's mother, has advanced part of the purchase money—provided

she did not intend it as a gift. This will also apply if the relative advanced money to extend or otherwise improve the house. That relative will then be entitled to a proportionate share on sale.

Legal Costs and Expenses

In the past, solicitors were obliged to charge a fixed fee when acting in the purchase or sale of a house, irrespective of the amount of work involved. This fee would increase on a sliding scale according to the value of the house. As from 1973, their fee is no longer fixed by the scale but must be 'fair and reasonable', ie based on the work involved. The intention is that both house buyer and seller should have cheaper legal fees, but this is not certain in all cases, because what is 'reasonable' is always open to argument. In practice the buyer could be charged more than the old scale fee, as would be likely if he bought for less than £5,000—say just a building plot, because the price involved is still a relevant consideration in fixing the legal fee.

Whilst many solicitors still hold to the scale charges, which they maintain are fair and reasonable in most cases, the important change from the client's point of view is that solicitors are now permitted to charge less; so it could be worthwhile shopping around. Once he knows the purchase price, a solicitor will usually be prepared to give a rough estimate of the total legal expenses.

Stamp Duty

In addition to legal expenses, the buyer must also pay stamp duty to the government on any house costing more than £15,000. (The seller need pay no stamp duty.) The table below gives the present rates of stamp duty and the old sliding scale of solicitors' charges; although the latter is no longer applicable, it may be used as a rule-of-thumb guide.

Basic Legal Costs

Price paid for house	*Stamp duty (payable by house buyer to government)*	*Old scale of solicitors' fixed charges**
£5,000	No stamp duty payable if the price	£67.50
£6,000	does not exceed £15,000	£75.00

Price paid for house	*Stamp duty (payable by house buyer to government)*	*Old scale of solicitors' fixed charges**
£7,000	Notice that stamp duty is payable as soon as the purchase price goes slightly beyond this figure, say to £15,100	£82.50
£8,000		£90.00
£9,000		£97.50
£10,000		£105.00
£11,000		£110.00
£12,000		£115.00
£13,000		£120.00
£14,000		£125.00
£15,000		£130.00
£15,100	£75.50	£130.50
£16,000	£80.00	£135.00
£17,000	£85.00	£140.00
£18,000	£90.00	£145.00
£19,000	£95.00	£150.00
£20,000	£100.00	£155.00
£22,000	£220.00	£165.00
£24,000	£240.00	£175.00
£25,000	£250.00	£180.00
£26,000	£390.00	£185.00
£28,000	£420.00	£195.00
£30,000	£450.00	£205.00
£31,000	£620.00	no fixed fee

Over £30,000, the stamp duty payable increases to £2 for every £100 of the purchase price.

* Until 1972 this scale used to apply to legal work done where title was not registered. Use it as a rough guide to see whether your solicitor's charges follow the new criteria of being 'fair and reasonable'.

Additional Costs

In addition to his stamp duty and legal costs on his purchase the buyer will normally have to pay an additional legal fee in respect of his building society mortgage. In an average case this would be about £40. There will also be minor items such as search fees and other out-of-pocket expenditure by the solicitor, which would amount to a further £10. If the buyer obtains his loan from an insurance company, or one of the lesser-known building societies, he may have to pay a further £40 or more in fees. This is because the lenders will usually want to employ separate solicitors. Do not underestimate the total extra expenses that may crop up when buying a house. Always keep £100 or so in hand, to cover unexpected items.

Some firms of solicitors are more expensive than others, simply because they work in more expensive areas and their overheads are higher. Nevertheless, it remains true that a solicitor's rate of charging is still basically related to the price of the house.

Objecting to a Legal Bill

A client who feels overcharged has a right to insist that the solicitor has his bill approved by his professional body, the Law Society. The society will give a certificate saying whether the amount charged is justified and, if excessive, will reduce it. (Obtaining a certificate will involve the solicitor in extra work, so he is likely to offer to reduce the bill, rather than to go to this trouble.)

Payment under Protest

Do not pay your bill if you think it is too high, because payment cancels the client's right to have it checked by the Law Society. If you have to make payment, write on your cheque, or in your covering letter, that it is made 'under protest'. You will then be entitled to a rebate if it is later shown that you have been overcharged.

Alternatively, the client can apply to a taxing master in the High Court to have his bill reduced. But this is generally not advisable, as the client will have to pay additional taxation costs if the taxing master thinks that the bill is fair or, at any rate, not excessive.

A House-owner's Rights

Restrictions

Even a freehold house or land may be subject to covenants which restrict how it can be used. For example, the owner may not be allowed to:

Use the land for any trade or business.

Keep poultry or animals.

Divide the house into flats.

In the case of a leasehold house and particularly a flat, the restrictions in the lease are likely to be far more numerous. Additionally the landlord can compel a leaseholder to repair and paint at regular intervals.

Town Planning Control on Development

Since 1947 any owner wishing to start building operations, or make any fundamental change in the way he has previously used his premises, eg from residential to business occupation, must obtain planning permission.

Interior Alterations

Interior alterations are not normally regarded as development. Thus, without permission, an owner may knock down internal walls in his home, perhaps to convert it into an open-plan house. On the other hand he may not divide the house up into separate residential units, unless planning permission is first obtained.

Minor External Alterations

An owner may enlarge or improve his house, or erect a garage, provided he does not increase the size of the house substantially, usually by not more than one-tenth. These regulations are complicated and subject to change from year to year, so every owner should check with his local town planning department, and not just rely on local rumour, eg assurances that his builder may give. The town planning department will also advise on minor regulations such as that the garage must not project beyond the line of the existing building.

Business Use

The general rule about using one's home for business purposes is that planning permission is needed only if the proposed business use is 'substantial'. Without permission an owner may:

Take in a small number of lodgers, provided this does not extend to turning the house into a guest-house.

Give private tuition at home, though he may not hold classes.

Hold nursery playgroups, provided that not more than six children are cared for on a paying basis; but the housewife, or whoever is in charge, should obtain the consent of the local welfare department, since in law she will be acting as a 'child minder'.

Provided he employs no one, an owner may carry on any genuine hobby—however lucrative a sideline, such as printing for friends. No advertising is allowed, and the owner must not put up any external advertisement. He should be certain his activity is a hobby only and not an extension of his business.

Small-scale Businesses

Suppose a house owner wants to start a small car-hire service. He needs no planning permission to operate it from home, provided it remains on a very small scale. But if his business grows, and he starts to use more than one car, he will need to apply for planning permission, which, in a residential area, is likely to be refused.

Enforcement Notices

The planning authority can put a stop to any unauthorised change of use by sending the householder an enforcement notice. If he does not stop within twenty-eight days, he can be prosecuted and heavily fined. In the meantime, it is still open to him to apply for planning permission, which, if granted, would regularise the change.

Applying for Planning Permission

The forms of application are readily available at the council offices. An owner who wants to carry out a major structural alteration or extension, will also have to submit detailed plans which are best prepared by an architect.

One way of avoiding expense initially is to apply for outline planning permission only, which will not necessitate detailed plans or measurements. Once outline permission is granted, this means that, in principle, the planning committee approves the alterations, and it will then be worthwhile employing an architect and spending money on more elaborate plans and detailed measurements.

The Architect

Even if only minor remodelling is planned, the services of an architect are usually worth the expense. His charges are normally on a sliding scale, between 6 and 10 per cent of the cost of the work, but the benefits—including legal safeguards—are considerable. For example:

He will draw up detailed plans and specifications in advance.

He will be able to keep the builders to their contract price, and prevent them running up costly extras.

His supervision will ensure that his client gets the quality of materials and workmanship that he has the right to expect.

An architect is responsible for his designs. For example, if the owner asks him to design an extension to be erected at a cost of £2,000, and no builder will undertake the work for less than £3,000, the owner is entitled to say that this is too expensive, and refuse to continue with the project. In this case, the architect would not be entitled to his design fee. On the other hand, if the owner makes use of the plans in a modified form, he would be obliged to pay a substantial portion of the design fee.

The architect is responsible for any construction he designs for six years after completion. If it begins to tilt or sag, this would indicate that his design was unsatisfactory, and he could be sued for negligence. After six years he is free from any liability, even if the building subsequently collapses. But the builder may be liable if collapse is due to a concealed defect.

Compulsory Purchase

It is common these days for a house-owner to lose his home because the local authority wants to pull it down to make way for a new housing development or road scheme. Many government bodies and state corporations have powers of compulsory purchase, and there is seldom much a private owner can do against them once the machinery is set in motion.

Where several house-owners are similarly affected, they can join together and start a publicity campaign against the scheme as a whole. (They may be able to contend, as part of their campaign at the public enquiry, that public money is being mis-spent.)

Compensation

Most owners will accept the inevitable, and concern themselves with that basic question—how much compensation will they get? One problem for the owner is the long delay, often several years, between confirmation of the scheme and the date when the authority actually takes the house. If, during this period, he wants to sell privately, he may find that it is difficult to realise what he thinks is a realistic figure. In these circumstances, the owner can insist that the authority buys his house immediately at the market value, which means the amount an owner would ordinarily expect to receive for his property if he put it up for sale on the open market.

Where only part of his land is taken he can claim compensation if the value of what remains has fallen. Or he can require the authority to buy the rest of his property.

The owner should always instruct an independent surveyor to negotiate the price on his behalf. The surveyor's fees, as well as legal fees and removal expenses, will be paid by the authority.

7 Renting Property

The Formalities of Renting

A tenant who proposes to take a lease for a period of over three years must ensure it is created by a formal deed. Without a deed his tenancy is likely to be declared invalid. To be a deed, the document must not only be signed by the landlord but must be 'signed, sealed and delivered' by him.

Normally sealing is achieved by affixing the customary small red seals used by lawyers, although any impression on the document suffices. The landlord 'delivers' the lease to the tenant. In return the tenant gives the landlord a copy called the counterpart signed and sealed by him.

Failure to observe these formalities may not render the lease entirely ineffective. A document which contains enough details of the proposed tenancy, may be regarded as a contract to grant a lease and might be enforceable as such by the courts.

Even in the absence of any document a tenant who has gone in and carried out repairs may be able to claim a lease in the courts.

Writing is not necessary where a lease is granted for three years or less provided the tenant is let into possession at once and pays the full market rent. A contract to grant a lease of any length to begin at a future date must be in writing to be enforceable.

Tenancies and Licences

An agreement for the occupation of premises may fall into one of the four categories detailed below.

1 *Fixed-term Tenancies.* These are tenancies lasting for a definite period, whether one week or several years. Normally such a tenancy cannot be terminated by either landlord or tenant before the end of the period.

2 *Periodic Tenancies.* A weekly, monthly or quarterly tenancy may be terminated by notice to quit served in accordance with the rules outlined below. If not so terminated, it automatically continues for a further period. A periodic tenancy sometimes arises when a tenant stays in possession after the end of a lease for a fixed term and continues to pay rent by reference to a certain period.

3 *Tenancies at Will.* These arise where a tenant occupies property on the understanding that he is to leave as soon as the landlord requires him to do so (although he has the right to re-enter for a reasonable time to remove his furniture and effects). It follows that there must be no definite period specified for the duration of the tenancy.

Tenancies at will often occur between relatives and friends, as when there is an informal arrangement to let the tenant stay in the property without paying rent. A tenant who remains in possession with the landlord's consent after the expiration of a fixed-term lease may become a tenant at will. This does not mean he can stay on rent free, since the landlord is entitled to compensation for use of the premises. If a regular rent is paid, this will point to a periodic tenancy but this is not necessarily conclusive. Similarly, there may sometimes be doubt as to whether there is a tenancy at will or a licence.

4 *Licences.* A licence gives a right to do one or more specific things on premises whereas a lease gives a general right to occupy premises (even though sometimes for a particular use only). The usual test in drawing this occasionally subtle distinction is whether the agreement gives a right to exclusive possession of the premises in question. If it does, there will be a tenancy. If it does not, there will be a licence. The question is often important in deciding whether someone is a lodger (and therefore a licensee) or a tenant.

Notice to Quit

A notice to quit must be in writing and 'in the prescribed form'. If there are no express terms in a lease dealing with notices to quit, the following rules apply:

1 A minimum of four weeks' clear notice is required to terminate the lease of *any* premises let as a dwelling.

2 Periodic tenancies (other than yearly tenancies) can be terminated by a clear notice of at least the period of the tenancy, expir-

ing on the last day of the current period or on the first day of any subsequent period.

3 Yearly tenancies can be terminated by clear notice of at least half a year. If a tenancy began on one of the usual quarter days (25 March, 24 June, 29 September or 25 December) half a year means two complete quarters. Otherwise, it means 182 days.

4 No period of notice is required to end a tenancy at will, not even the four-week period mentioned above.

'Clear notice' means that in calculating the period you must exclude the day on which the notice is sent (but not, if different, the day on which it is received) and the day on which it expires. The tenant is allowed to stay on in the premises until the end of the day in which the notice expires. If the notice does not clearly state the intention to terminate or the day on which the notice expires, it will be invalid.

Where there is some uncertainty from which day the period of the tenancy runs, difficulties can be avoided by using the following form of words: 'Notice to expire on a given date or on such other date as the period of your tenancy would expire being not less than four clear weeks following the date of the service upon you of this notice.'

Obligations under Tenancies

Certain obligations are regarded by the law as being basic to the relationship between landlord and tenant. These are therefore deemed to be incorporated in every tenancy, where they are not expressly excluded by the parties. Indeed, some of these implied covenants cannot be excluded even by express agreement.

Landlords' Implied Obligations

Under common law the landlord was obliged to compensate the tenant for any interference with the tenant's *quiet enjoyment*, ie undisturbed possession, of the property. This does not mean quiet enjoyment in the acoustic sense. The obligation is broken if the landlord cuts off his gas or electricity or tries to drive him out by persistent threats.

But there was no implied obligation on the landlord to do repairs save in the case of a furnished letting where there was an implied condition that the premises were fit for human habitation when let.

However, social legislation has imposed further requirements on landlords. Thus, in leases of houses where the rent is under £80 a year in London, or £52 elsewhere, there is an implied covenant that the landlord will keep the premises fit for human habitation throughout the tenancy.

More important is the Housing Act, 1961, which applies to houses and flats both humble and expensive which are let for less than seven years. There is an implied covenant by the landlord to maintain the outside of the house and the water, gas, electricity, sanitation and heating installations.

The landlord is liable only for defects of which he is made aware but he cannot get the tenant to take over this basic responsibility.

Under the Defective Premises Act, 1972, a landlord who is obliged or entitled to enter to carry out repairs owes a duty to ensure that everyone using or visiting the building is reasonably safe from injury or damage to his belongings.

Tenants' Implied Obligations

Apart from his obligation to pay the rent, the tenant is under no implied obligation to do repairs. Nevertheless, he is bound to treat the premises with reasonable care, and to prevent damage to it. Although a tenant has not undertaken to carry out repairs (as often happens where he holds on a weekly or monthly basis) he 'must take proper care of the place. He must clean the chimneys and windows. He must mend the electric light when it fuses. He must unstop the sink when it is blocked by waste.' If his family or guests do damage he must repair it. Liability for failing to repair is normally dealt with by specific agreement, but it may be that neither the landlord nor the tenant is responsible for particular repairs if the point is not covered by the lease.

Express Covenants

Among the express covenants often contained in leases are the following:

Covenant by Tenant Not to Assign or Sub-let. In the absence of any prohibition a tenant (other than a tenant at will) is free to transfer his lease to a new tenant or to sub-let all or part of the premises. Naturally, if there is an outright covenant not to assign or sub-let, that is the end of the matter.

If the lease states merely that the tenant is not to assign or sub-let *without the landlord's consent*, then the landlord is not allowed to withhold consent unreasonably. The parties to the lease cannot themselves define what grounds for refusal are reasonable. That is for the court to decide.

It should also be noted that taking in a lodger is not a breach of the covenant against sub-letting.

Liability of Tenant under His Covenant to Repair. Clearly, the division of responsibility for repairs will depend upon the terms of each lease. A covenant by the tenant to 'repair' or 'keep in repair' implies a covenant to *put* the premises into a normal standard of repair. It is therefore essential that the tenant should find out, before taking on the lease, just how much expenditure may be involved since if he takes the lease of a house or flat which is in poor repair he will have to put it into good repair at his own expense, even though the lease refers only to *keeping* it in repair.

Repairs can involve the tenant in heavy expense. Oddly enough, in law the standard of repair required can vary from one property to another. The character and also the locality of the house or flat will affect the standard to be expected: If you rent a mansion in Mayfair, you will have to repair it to a higher standard than if you rent a terraced house in Hackney.

Also, the age of the house will be relevant. This is a complex consideration. On the one hand the tenant must keep it in what is reasonably good condition for a building of that age. This may involve him in a good deal of renewal. He may, over the years, find himself having to replace part after part until the whole building has virtually been renewed. On the other hand, no landlord can insist that he carries renewal to the point of reconstruction and hands back a completely renovated home when he goes.

Admittedly, if a wall is dangerous, he must rebuild it, but if the foundations of a house are found to be defective, the tenant will not be obliged to renew them. Again, he would not have to renew or rebuild the property under his repairing covenant if it is damaged or destroyed by fire, storm or bombing or like calamity. The landlord has to cover this by insurance, but can make the tenant pay the premium.

The strictness of the tenant's repairing obligation can be lessened by having 'fair wear and tear excepted'. A solicitor acting for a tenant will have done well if he persuades the landlord to accept this qualification.

As a result, the tenant will not have to repair, say, a floor or staircase, which has worn away by the constant passage of feet. But if wear is so great that some parts have actually broken, he will have to replace these.

There are, in practice, numerous statutory restrictions curbing the power of a landlord to enforce his tenant's strict repairing obligation. For example, in the case of very old premises which have almost run their life span, the Landlord and Tenant Act, 1927, frees a tenant from his obligation to pay compensation for defects in repair if the premises are to be pulled down, or such structural alterations made that any repairs would, in fact, be pointless.

Again, the Leasehold Property (Repair) Act, 1938, protects a tenant who has a long lease—of seven years or more. It prevents the landlord claiming damages for non-repair until the lease nears its end. Generally, he cannot enforce the covenant to repair or ask for compensation unless there are less than three years left to run.

Tenant's Covenant Relating to the Use of the Premises. The lease of any residential property usually contains restrictions against carrying on any trade or business, although certain professions are often accepted. There will also be a covenant against 'illegal or immoral uses', which might cover, for example, gambling or prostitution.

Covenants in Leases of Flats. Leases of flats, particularly those in large, purpose-built blocks, often contain very detailed covenants and restrictions relating to such matters as noise and pets, in addition to delimiting obligations concerning repair, decorations and services. Under such leases there will be an obligation on the landlord to keep the common parts in repair, eg the lifts and communal roof. For details of the landlord's liability to visitors using such common parts, see Chapter 8.

Liability under Covenants

It is not always appreciated that each of the *original* parties to a lease remains liable to the other under the covenants for the duration of the lease. This is so even after the original tenant has sold his leasehold interest or the original landlord has parted with the reversion.

A purchaser from the original tenant is liable only so long as he retains the lease. However, where a lease is assigned for value, there is an implied covenant by the incoming tenant to the outgoing tenant not to breach the terms of the lease.

Naturally, court proceedings on a breach of covenant will normally be brought against the tenant for the time being; but if, for instance, he is unable to pay the damages awarded, the original tenant may be exposed to a claim. The moral is that when selling leases ensure the new tenant will be capable of paying the rent and not likely to break the terms laid down by the lease.

Remedies for Breach of Covenant

The remedies of damages and injunction to restrain a breach of covenant are available.

Rarely a tenant might get an order for specific performance against a landlord who has failed to comply with his covenant to repair, but not vice-versa.

A landlord can sue his tenant for unpaid rent in the same way as for any other debt.

Two further remedies are sometimes open to the landlord:

1 *Distress for rent.* If rent is in arrears, the landlord has the right to seize or 'distrain' the tenant's goods and either hold them as security for payment or sell them and keep the proceeds. The landlord must not take goods which are clearly worth more than the outstanding rent and if he sells the goods he must account to the tenant for any surplus. Certain of the tenant's goods, such as loose money, clothing, bedding and tools up to the value of £50 cannot be seized. (This £50 limit can be increased at some future time to meet inflation.)

If the landlord takes property found on the premises which belongs to some third party, it is up to that third party to give a notice in writing to the landlord in order to prevent the landlord from selling and in order to reclaim his goods. If he fails to give notice and his goods are sold, his only recourse will be against the tenants.

Distress will normally be carried out by duly certified bailiffs, but they are not permitted to break in for this purpose. The consent of the court is required before goods are seized if the tenancy is subject to the Rent Acts (see p 99).

2 *Forfeiture.* Most leases specify that the landlord can terminate the lease and take back the property in the event of non-payment of rent or other breaches of covenant.

Before the landlord can bring a court action for forfeiture for a breach of covenant (excluding non-payment of rent) he must first serve a written notice on the tenant which must specify the alleged breach of covenant, ask the tenant to put it right (if possible) and state any compensation which is claimed. If the tenant fails either to remedy the breach or to pay compensation within a reasonable time, the landlord can commence forfeiture proceedings. Where the covenant in question relates only to decorative repair, or where the lease is of at least seven years with at least three years to run, the court will only allow forfeiture in certain circumstances, eg if the value of the landlord's reversion is being seriously affected by the breach of covenant.

Apart from this restriction, the court has a general discretion to refuse to allow forfeiture. But even if a court order is obtained for non-payment of rent, the tenant can still save the lease by paying the rent within twenty-eight days of the order.

Leases and Moving

An Englishman's home may be his castle but this does not mean he can always sell it. What is its asset value if he holds only a lease? Saleability depends on the clause in the lease dealing with assignment.

If there is no written agreement, or the tenancy agreement does not forbid assignment, the landlord cannot prevent it. But every assignment must be by deed, although generally an informal document will be accepted by the court.

Leases granted for more than three years are usually worded so as to permit an assignment with the landlord's consent. If so the landlord cannot unreasonably withhold his consent and must allow the premises to be taken over by a new tenant who is respectable and responsible.

A lease for less than three years will usually ban assignment and sub-letting, which means that the tenant may not transfer occupation to anyone else or sub-let in any circumstances. In this case the tenant has virtually nothing to sell and, if he decides to move, can only offer to hand back his home to his landlord. This is invariably the position if the lease is on a monthly or quarterly basis.

The Rent Act

An unexpected obstacle to selling one's flat may be the provisions of the Rent Act. While the lease itself may permit an assignment and so in law be freely transferable, the Rent Act makes it illegal for the tenant to demand a cash sum for it. Indeed, the Rent Act prohibits his getting even a benefit in kind from the incoming tenant. Usually the only compensation an outgoing tenant can claim is a portion of what he has actually paid for improvements and then only at a low valuation.

Admittedly there is a loophole in the law whereby the outgoing tenant can receive a profit payment from the incoming tenant, but this depends on the landlord allowing a fresh lease to be granted. Instead of assigning the remainder of the lease, he is allowed to surrender it to the landlord on condition he grants a fresh lease to the new tenant. There is nothing in the Acts prohibiting the outgoing tenant asking for a cash consideration for the surrender of his lease.

Regarding fixtures and fittings, an outgoing tenant is allowed to charge the new tenant what he himself has spent in structural alterations and fixtures which he cannot take away. But he must draw up an inventory. If he overcharges the new tenant for fixtures or furniture he is guilty of an offence. Here the local authority can, under the Act, inspect and advise the new tenant on valuation, but few tenants know this or even that they can claim this money back from the outgoing tenant if they have been overcharged.

Recently a tenant contracted to sell the lease of his flat; £3,750 was to be paid for furniture actually worth £600. The judge compelled the tenant to assign the lease for £600—deducting the £3,150 excess which was an illegal premium.

The Rent Acts

Historically, the common law has been weighted in favour of the landlord. However, the social legislation of this century has strengthened the position of many tenants.

Protection under the Rent Acts is given to both furnished and unfurnished accommodation and includes any house or flat with a rateable value of £750 or less; in the London area the limit is raised to £1,500. This means that all but the most expensive accommodation is subject to some form of rent control. Even tenants who do not qualify for full protection as 'regulated' tenants may still be able to apply to the Rent Tribunal for limited security or to have their rent reduced.

Regulated Tenancies

Unfurnished Accommodation. To qualify for protection as a regulated tenancy the following conditions must be satisfied:

1 The rent payable must not be less than two-thirds of the rateable value.

2 The tenant must not be *sharing* living accommodation with the landlord. There is no hard-and-fast rule as to what constitutes living accommodation: a kitchen would generally be regarded as living accommodation whereas a bathroom normally would not. It does not matter if living accommodation is shared with anyone other than the landlord.

3 The tenancy must be purely residential. If part of the premises is used for business purposes, the entire letting is outside the Rent Acts. (There are separate rules protecting tenants of business premises.)

New Protection for Furnished Tenants. Since 1974 many furnished tenants have become regulated which means they have the same protection as unfurnished tenants, provided that the following conditions are satisfied:

That the landlord does not live on the premises.

That the landlord does not provide any board or breakfast, or personal services such as cleaning or washing of clothes or bed-linen.

That the accommodation is not a students' hostel or holiday accommodation.

Fair Rent. No regulated tenant can be made to pay more than a fair rent. Whilst a tenant is still free to agree to any rent for a tenancy to which the Rent Acts apply, he may at any time apply to the rent officer employed by the local authority for a 'fair rent' to be registered. If the decision of the rent officer is not acceptable to both landlord and tenant, either can then appeal before a rent assessment committee. This, too, is independent, with a lawyer as chairman, a surveyor, and a lay member.

A fair rent is based on the hypothetical assumption that there is no scarcity of accommodation in the area. This means that the notion of a market rent is excluded. The rent officer must take into account the state of repair of the accommodation, its age and character. The locality and other relevant circumstances must also be considered. But not the provision of any new amenity or improvement in the neighbourhood nor any deterioration in the amenities of the neighbourhood. He will, of course, make a comparison with similar lettings in the area for which a fair rent has already been assessed. He must ignore any personal circumstances of either landlord or tenant, but will take into account all services provided by the landlord.

It may be that the tenant has made improvements over and above his legal obligations. These are not taken into account but the rent officer would generally assess at a lower figure than if the landlord had carried out the improvements. Similarly, the rent officer will not take into account any disrepair due to the tenant's own failure to comply with his obligations under his agreement. Here the landlord is obviously not at fault, and there would be no reason for reducing the assessment.

Where furnished tenants have full protection and are subject to the fair-rent procedure, the circumstances considered in determining a fair rent are extended to include the quantity, quality and condition of furniture. But the rent officer must disregard any deterioration in the condition of furniture due to ill-treatment by the tenant.

Once assessed, the rent is registered and remains the maximum that can be charged until it is revoked or varied or altered by the rent assessment committee on appeal. An application to change it cannot normally be made until three years after the date of the last registration, save on the ground that it is no longer a fair rent, for example if the landlord has made improvements to the premises.

An application to a rent officer to fix a fair rent may be made on the prescribed form available from the local authority, either by the landlord or the tenant, or sometimes by the local authority itself, where a tenant applies for a rent allowance. On it the applicant must propose the rent that he suggests is fair, and it is up to the rent officer to decide whether he agrees with it.

Sometimes the landlord invites the tenant to make an application jointly with him for registration of a fair rent. The danger here for the tenant is that if the rent officer considers the rent proposed in a joint application fair, no appeal is permitted to the rent assessment committee. Again, no appeal is allowed if the rent officer accepts as fair the rent proposed by the landlord, unless the tenant has made a representation in writing against the amount proposed.

Where the rent officer is not satisfied that the rent specified in the application is a fair rent, or if the tenant challenges it in writing, the rent officer must call a hearing. This involves an informal meeting called a consultation, at which the tenant does not need to be represented by a professional person such as a lawyer or surveyor.

However, if there is an appeal to the rent-assessment committee, any tenant of limited means can apply for assistance at a nominal charge under the surveyors' aid scheme, forms for which are available through any citizens' advice bureau. In practice, the average tenant can get skilled help most cheaply by joining a tenants' association.

Nature of a Regulated Tenancy. A regulated tenant is often referred to as 'the statutory tenant', because his occupation is protected by statute after his lease runs out or after a notice to quit has expired. He cannot be evicted save under the provisions of the Rent Acts. *His 'tenancy' is really a personal right* which he cannot leave by will or sell to anyone else. It comes to an end if he gives up possession of the premises.

When the tenant dies, the tenancy passes to his widow, if she was living with him when he died. Otherwise, the tenancy may be inherited by any member of his family (including a 'common law' spouse as well as quite distant relatives and in-laws) who was living with him at least six months before his death. When the new tenant dies, there can be a second transmission to one of *his* relatives, but there can be no further transmission on the third death.

How a Landlord Can Obtain Possession

Discretionary Grounds

The following are the grounds on which a possession order may be granted (subject always to the court's discretion and the overriding consideration of reasonableness).

1 If suitable alternative accommodation is available to the tenant. If a landlord obtains a certificate from a local housing authority that such is the case, the condition is satisfied. Otherwise the landlord must show that he or someone else will provide accommodation which is comparable so far as rent, security of tenure, nearness to the tenant's work, etc, are concerned.

2 If there has been a breach of covenant by the tenant or he has failed to pay his rent. The court will in such cases often make a suspended order, giving the tenant time to pay the rent.

3 If the tenant has caused a nuisance or annoyance to his neighbours or has used the premises for illegal or immoral purposes.

4 If the tenant is responsible for the deterioration of the premises or, if furnished, of the furniture.

5 If the tenant has given notice to quit and the landlord, in reliance on it, has contracted to sell or let the premises, so as to be seriously prejudiced.

6 If the tenant has assigned or sub-let the whole of the premises without the landlord's permission.

7 If the premises are reasonably required by the landlord for the occupation of an employee. This applies only if the premises were let to the tenant as a result of *his* employment by the landlord.

8 If the premises are reasonably required by the landlord for occupation by himself, an adult child, his parents or parents-in-law. The court cannot grant possession for this reason if the landlord became the landlord as a result of a purchase after 23 March 1965 (ie if the tenant was already in residence). This will not affect a landlord who bought a house after that date and subsequently let it. The court must not grant possession if this would cause greater hardship to the tenant than its refusal would to the landlord.

9 If the tenant has sub-let part of the premises under a sublease to which the Rent Acts apply and is receiving an excessive rent.

Non-discretionary Grounds

In the following instances the court is bound to grant possession when the landlord requires it.

1 Where an owner-occupier has given *written notice* before the tenant goes into occupation, that the owner intends to re-occupy, eg after returning from an overseas post.

2 An owner who intends to retire to a house or bungalow can let it in the meantime. He must give *written notice* before the tenant moves in, that he will want to live there himself on retirement.

3 Holiday accommodation can be safely let out of season for a fixed period of up to eight months provided the landlord has given *written notice* that he will want the house for holiday letting in the season.

4 Where an educational institution lets to a student for a fixed term of not more than twelve months.

Powers of the Rent Tribunal

A tenant who shares living accommodation with his landlord has no automatic security of tenure under the Rent Acts, but he can apply to the rent tribunal. So, too, can a furnished tenant whose landlord lives in the same building.

The protection of the rent tribunals extend to those furnished tenants who do not qualify for full protection under the Rent Act, 1974. They can grant limited protection to all save the most temporary accommodation. But where substantial board is provided in addition to accommodation, they have no jurisdiction.

The chief power of the rent tribunal lies in the fact that it can suspend the operation of a notice to quit for up to six months. This means that if the members of the tribunal sympathise with the tenant they can postpone the date on which he has to give up possession. Moreover, once the tenant has received an initial period of security he can come back again.

The position is that provided he behaves himself, complies with his obligations, and does not annoy the neighbours, an unprotected furnished tenant's security may be continually extended for an indefinite sequence of six-monthly periods.

However, the tribunal has still no power to grant security if the landlord formerly occupied the accommodation himself and wants it back to live there again, or for a member of his family, provided the tenant had written warning of this when he took the tenancy. In practice, of course, a tenant can generally stay on until the landlord gets a court order for possession, since eviction without a court order is unlawful and could amount to the crime of harassment.

The other function of the rent tribunal will continue to be fixing rents for those remaining categories of furnished lettings which do not qualify for full protection under the new Rent Act. The fixing of rents has generally meant reducing those thought to be excessive. Their decision is recorded in a register of rents kept by the local authority, which anyone may inspect. A landlord who tries to charge more than the registered rent or charge a premium can be prosecuted.

Where a tenant has been guilty of misbehaviour, such as causing a nuisance to neighbours, the tribunal may reduce the period of security.

General Rules on Eviction and Harassment

A county court order is required before a landlord can take possession of premises, even if a tenancy has ended. This applies also to the landlord's rights of forfeiture. If the landlord tries to take possession without a court order or if he tries to make the tenant leave by, for example, cutting off gas and electricity, he is guilty of a criminal offence.

Surrender to Landlord

All this is not to say that a protected tenant can never turn his asset into hard cash. There is nothing in the Rent Act which makes it unlawful for a landlord to offer him a sum of money in return for giving up his tenancy and, in fact, this is frequently done. But his agreement to leave is not enforceable should the tenant change his mind and refuse to go.

In those circumstances it may be difficult for the landlord to get his money back. What is usually arranged is for the sum offered to be placed in a bank account in the joint names of their respective solicitors. They will release the money only when he has moved out.

Prohibition on 'Key Money'

Clearly it would be an evasion of rent control if the landlord could charge a lump sum or premium at the start of the tenancy in addition to rent. Under the Rent Acts, a landlord is not permitted to demand a premium as well as rent and to do so is an offence punishable by a fine. Nevertheless, a tenant who pays key money is not breaking the law himself and can, after taking occupation, claim it back. By so doing, he does not lose his protected tenancy.

Sometimes a landlord may try to disguise a premium by calling it 'a loan' or by insisting that the prospective tenant buys furniture at an inflated price. Here the tenant can claim back what he has paid over and above the true worth of the furniture. Since a landlord who sells furniture to a tenant must give him an inventory showing the price of each item, this should not be too difficult to ascertain and in any case the local authority can give a valuation.

8 About the House

Occupier's Liability

The occupier of every property owes a duty of care to all lawful visitors not to allow either the condition of the premises or anything done on the premises to cause them harm. The word 'occupier' has a wide sense and includes anyone in control of premises. For instance, a landlord of a block of flats is usually 'the occupier' of any common parts such as the lifts, for which he is responsible under the lease. Lawful visitors include not only persons actually invited by the occupier but also persons impliedly permitted to come on to his property. For example, a door-to-door salesman will normally be a lawful visitor. However, if there is a notice on the front garden gate clearly stating 'No Hawkers', he may well be regarded as a trespasser. Moreover, if he strays off the garden path and goes into a part of the property in which he would not be entitled to assume he was allowed to go, he may again be treated as a trespasser. Persons with a legal right of entry in some circumstances, such as the police or meter readers, are also lawful visitors, whether the occupier consents to their visit or not.

How Much Care Need an Occupier Take?

The rule of law is simply that an occupier must take reasonable steps to ensure that his property is reasonably safe for lawful visitors going about the purpose for which they are allowed on to the property. He must allow for the fact that children are less able to look after themselves than adults (see also Chapter 4). On the other hand, a person with some professional skill is expected to cope with any difficulties which arise out of his work. Obviously, these are very general principles and every case turns very much on its particular facts. However, the following are illustrations of how these principles have been applied:

1 A fishmonger who was delivering fish to a customer was invited in for a cup of tea. As he was leaving, a door handle came away in his hand, causing him to fall several feet from an unrailed platform. The handle had been fixed by the customer himself. The court held that the customer had discharged his duty of care to his visitor by exercising the degree of skill and care which a reasonably skilled carpenter might have done in the reasonable belief that the handle would be secure. The fishmonger lost his case.

2 The manager of a public house was allowed by the brewers who owned it to take in paying guests in his private quarters. As a result of the manager leaving the stairs unlit, a guest fell downstairs and was fatally injured. In law the brewers were 'the occupiers', so it was they who were sued. However, the court held that the brewers could not reasonably have foreseen that the manager would have left the staircase unlit, and they were therefore not liable.

3 A six-year-old girl climbed a low wall surrounding flowers which were lit up by lights beneath thin, coloured glass. Although ordered off three times, she was not warned about the glass through which she fell, injuring herself. The court ruled that the child could not be expected to think of the added danger of the glass and that she was entitled to damages.

4 A window-cleaner was in the habit of steadying himself when working at a particular house by holding on to a plywood pane in which a hole had been cut for a ventilator. The owner of the house, unaware of this habit, removed the bolts holding the pane to the window frame. As a result, the window-cleaner was injured. He sued the owner of the house. The court held that it was up to the window-cleaner to satisfy himself as to the safety or condition of the premises in which he was to work. Accordingly, the house owner was not liable.

Warning the Visitor

It is sometimes thought that an occupier sufficiently discharges his duty of care by putting up a notice or giving a verbal warning to his visitor. This may not always be sufficient. For instance, if the occupier could have taken steps to reduce the danger but contented himself with a warning, he may still be liable. A notice may also be less of a defence where the injury in question resulted from some positive action by the occupier rather than from the static condition of the premises. However, if it can be shown that the visitor was fully aware of and voluntarily accepted the risk, the occupier may escape all liability. The principle of contributory negligence (see Chapter 1) is also applicable in this area of the law and may result in a reduction of damages recoverable.

Independent Contractors

If an occupier arranges for reputable professional contractors to carry out work for him, he will usually not be liable for any damage or injury caused through faulty workmanship on their part. Thus, if a householder has his roof repaired by professional builders who leave a loose slate which later falls on a visitor's head, he will probably not be liable—though the contractor may be.

Occupier's Responsibility on Adjoining Highway

An occupier is also liable for injuries to people on the highway beside the house, and in such cases having employed an independent contractor is not a defence if necessary precautions are not taken. The legal principles set out below (in the section on interference with one's neighbours) are also relevant in this context.

Liability to Trespassers

A trespasser is someone who, innocently or not, is on someone else's land without that person's express or implied consent. An occupier's liability to a trespasser for injury, for which a lawful visitor could bring an action, depends on what the courts in modern cases have called his general 'humanitarian duty'. This requirement is less demanding on the occupier than the duty of care owed to lawful visitors.

The distinction between injuries arising out of the condition of the premises and injuries arising out of the positive actions of the occupiers is particularly important in the case of trespassers. So is the distinction between adult and child trespassers. An occupier must bear in mind that there may be something on his property which is both an attraction and a danger to children. He must then take steps to minimise the risk of injury to children even though they are trespassers. Furthermore, an occupier must recognise that mere warnings are insufficient to safeguard a child trespasser.

Interfering with One's Neighbours

The classic problem of holding a fair balance between each man's right to do what he likes in his own home and his neighbour's right not to be disturbed by this is not easily reduced to a few legal principles. The ways in which one neighbour may annoy another are almost infinite. However, the law has categorised them as far as possible into the following four classes:

Physical encroachment on to a neighbour's land.

Physical damage to a neighbour's land.

Interference with the enjoyment of a neighbour's land by noise, smells or otherwise.

Escape of anything dangerous kept on the owner's land.

In the case of physical encroachment on to a neighbour's land, there is theoretically no need for the neighbour to prove any actual damage in order for him to seek a legal remedy. However, he would in practice be most ill-advised to do so unless he had suffered damage. Interference with the enjoyment of a neighbour's land by noise, smells, etc, can only be legally actionable if the person causing the annoyance can be shown to be acting unreasonably. One factor in deciding this is the character of the neighbourhood. In the words of a Victorian judge, 'What would be a nuisance in Belgrave Square would not necessarily be so in Bermondsey.' Other relevant factors include the intentions of the person committing the alleged nuisance and how long the nuisance lasts. It is no ground for complaint that the person suffering is particularly sensitive to the nuisance. The nuisance must be such as to interfere seriously with a normal man's reasonable enjoyment of his property.

One particular kind of nuisance which falls into this category is the deprivation of light. The expression 'ancient lights' is the popular term for the prescriptive right to light. Generally, such a right can be obtained by twenty years' uninterrupted, undisputed and open use of light. Moreover, the right can attach only to a particular window or other opening designed to let in light. It cannot be enjoyed by a building as a whole, nor by a garden or other open space.

Each neighbour has a right to support for his land from adjoining land, but in the absence of any express covenants or agreements there is no automatic right of support for buildings. However, such a right can be acquired by twenty years' enjoyment.

If a person collects on his land anything likely to cause damage should it escape on to other land, that person will be liable even if he can show that he took reasonable precautions. This rule is limited to cases where the collection of anything dangerous is regarded as not part of the natural use of the land. This legal rule has been applied to many different substances, including electricity, sewage, explosives, fire and water. However, there is no liability for a fire which starts accidentally, unless its subsequent spread is the result of negligence.

It is a defence that there was no possible precaution which could have prevented the accident. This is known as the 'act of God' defence.

Household Pets

Dangerous and Non-dangerous Animals

Although the law relating to liability for damage caused by animals has recently been codified by statute, it remains full of fine distinctions between different kinds of animals. The chief division is between dangerous and non-dangerous animals. An animal is regarded as dangerous if it belongs to a species which is not commonly domesticated in the British Isles and is of such a nature that fully grown animals of the species are likely, unless restrained, to cause severe damage to persons or property, or that any damage they do cause is likely to be severe.

It is important to note that the classification 'dangerous' is conclusive. The temperament of the individual animal is irrelevant.

This definition clearly excludes cats and dogs. It also excludes creatures such as rabbits and pigeons which are 'commonly domesticated' in this country, although the majority of their species are wild. There is still some doubt as to how the recently introduced statutory rules will classify more exotic pets, such as monkeys.

Absolute Liability

It is not illegal to keep a dangerous animal as a pet but the keeper is invariably liable for any damage caused by it, however much care he has taken, whether or not he knew that the animal was dangerous and whether or not the damage was caused by the misbehaviour of the animal. In Lord Devlin's vivid illustration: 'If a person wakes up in the middle of the night and finds an escaping tiger on top of his bed and suffers a heart attack, it would be nothing to the point that the intentions of the tiger were quite amiable.' This kind of unqualified liability is known as 'absolute liability'.

Most household pets will belong to non-dangerous species. A keeper of such an animal will be 'absolutely' liable for damages caused by it only if the damage is of a kind which the animal was likely to cause unless restrained or if any damage that the animal might cause was likely to be severe. Secondly, it is necessary that this likelihood was due to characteristics of the individual animal which are not normally found in the species (except perhaps at particular times or in particular circumstances). Thirdly, the keeper of the animal must have known of its particular tendencies. (If the animal is the pet of a child under sixteen, who knew of the animal's disposition, the head of the house—if he is the keeper—is presumed also to have known.)

The 'First Bite' Principle

The effect of these rules is that animals of a non-dangerous species are presumed to be harmless unless there is contrary evidence. From this arises the well-known rule of a dog being allowed its 'first bite', a principle which is well illustrated by the following case:

A man was bitten twice by the same dog within half an hour. He failed to receive damages for the first bite but succeeded over the second, as by that time the dog's owner had had time to put the animal under control after it had revealed its aggressive character.

If the three conditions, set out above for non-dangerous animals, are satisfied, the keeper of the animal will again be liable for damage whether or not he can show that he took reasonable steps to keep the animal under control. If all the conditions are not satisfied, he may still be liable for damage done by the animal to someone to whom the keeper owed a duty of care, but in such cases it will be a defence that reasonable precautions had been taken. This may arise where the animal is allowed on to a public highway without supervision.

Dogs

There are some special rules of law relating solely to dogs. The most important of these is that the keeper of a dog which kills or injures livestock is liable, irrespective of whether this is the dog's first offence. A farmer, for example, is entitled to kill a dog if he has reasonable grounds for thinking that it is about to attack his livestock, but he must report the incident to the police within forty-eight hours.

Protecting One's Property

Trespassers

The limited duty of care which a householder owes to a trespasser has been described above. A householder is permitted to take reasonable steps to discourage trespassers, but he is not allowed deliberately to make his property dangerous to them.

If a trespasser refuses to leave his property after being told to do so, the householder is entitled to use reasonable force to eject him. However, the use of any force more than is necessary to remove the trespasser may constitute an assault.

If a householder is confronted by squatters on his property, it is illegal for him to force an entrance in order to eject them. Even so, it appears that if an owner obtains entry to the house by peaceful means he is entitled to try to throw out the squatters if they refuse his request to leave, as though they were ordinary trespassers (as in preceding paragraph), but in practice a court order should be sought. Apart from their civil liability as trespassers, squatters commit a criminal offence if they physically resist efforts to eject them, even if they themselves entered by peaceful means.

If a trespasser causes any damage, he is liable for the amount by which the value of the land is reduced. However, it is not necessary for any actual damage to have occurred in order to sue a trespasser: the mere act of trespassing makes him liable in damages (see also Chapter 7 in this connection).

So far as other intruders (such as burglars) are concerned, one is entitled to use reasonable force to protect one's property, but not to inflict serious injury or cause risk to life.

9 Libel and Slander

The Nature of Defamation

Defamation is the communication to another of a statement about a third person which tends to damage that person's reputation, or cause other people to avoid him or her. Such communication is usually referred to as 'publication': in this context, the word may mean not only publication in a book or newspaper but, for example, a letter or conversation. It is enough for the statement to be 'published' to just one other person, even just the husband or wife of the victim of the defamation.

The act of communication must be either deliberate or the result of negligence. For instance, if the statement leaks out because of an unforeseen violation of privacy, its originator will not be liable.

The statement itself can be in any form. Though it will usually be in words, either spoken or written, this is not always so: a gesture, a picture or any other form of communication may convey a defamatory message.

The reputation which the law is willing to protect is that in which a citizen is held by the man in the street and not by any particular section of society.

A statement may be defamatory if it tends to cause a person to be socially shunned, even if it does not imply anything morally reprehensible. For instance, an allegation that a person is insane or suffering from a contagious disease may be defamatory.

A statement may have only one obvious meaning or it may be possible to infer another meaning from it. In either case, if without knowledge of any special circumstances not mentioned in the statement, a reasonable man will draw a defamatory meaning from the statement, it will be defamatory. However, it is not permissible to stretch the interpretation of the statement so as to arrive at a defamatory meaning.

Innuendo

Whether or not a statement, by itself, is overtly or impliedly defamatory, it may become so if linked to particular facts known to those to whom it is published. An action may be brought on the basis of such an 'innuendo', perhaps in addition to any claims founded on other defamatory meanings which can be read into the statement by itself. Yet again, the question at issue is whether a reasonable man would infer a defamatory meaning in the light of the relevant facts.

Obviously, it is essential for a plaintiff to show that the statement could be taken as referring to him. Frequently, the outcome of defamation actions turns on this point.

If a statement refers to a group of people, it will not usually be possible for any member of the group to sue unless the group is well defined and the statement clearly refers to each and every member, without exception. Naturally, it would be different if the statement could be shown to single out one or more particular members of the group.

Who Is Liable?

Not only the originator of a statement but everyone who repeats it, or is in any way party to its dissemination, is *prima facie* liable. The most obvious example of this is a newspaper article. The author, the editor, the printer, the publisher and in some cases even the newsagents who distribute the newspaper can be sued. However, people like newsagents who play only a secondary role in publication can escape liability if they can show that they did not know and had no reason to know that they were disseminating defamatory matter.

Defences

There are five principal grounds on which a defence may be based against an accusation of defamation.

1 *Justification.* It is a complete defence to a suit for defamation that the statement complained of is true. This is known as the defence of 'justification'. Naturally, if a statement has more than one meaning it is necessary to establish the truth of the particular meaning complained of. This defence is not available if the defamation relates to a criminal conviction which under the Rehabilitation of Offenders

Act, 1974, is a 'spent' offence (ie one that is officially 'struck off the record') and if the publication is proved to have been made with malice.

2 *Fair Comment.* If a defendant can show that his statement was fair comment on a matter of public interest, he will not be liable. It is essential that the facts on which the comment is made are true, unless the comment is in a statement made on a *privileged* occasion (see below). The facts must also be of public interest. In other words, they must relate to the public acts of people in public life, or to the workings of institutions which are of importance to the community. Obviously, the details of someone's private life may be of interest to members of the public, but they will not be of public interest in the required sense.

A comment must also be 'fair'. This adjective is perhaps misleading. It does not mean that the comment has to be impartial or in accordance with the views to be expected of a reasonable man. On the contrary, the defence can still succeed even if the comment is a prejudiced, minority view. What is essential is that it should be honest. If, therefore, it can be demonstrated that the defendant was moved by personal dislike of the plaintiff (usually referred to as 'express malice') the defence will not be available.

3 *Privilege.* As a matter of public policy, the law gives immunity in certain circumstances to anyone making a statement, however defamatory it would otherwise be. This immunity is known as 'privilege'. There are two degrees of privilege, 'absolute' and 'qualified'.

If someone has the benefit of absolute privilege, he cannot be sued for defamation whatever he says and whatever his motives may be. Absolute privilege is enjoyed by members of either House of Parliament for statements made in Parliament. Reports published at the order of either House are similarly covered. It also protects all statements in court made by anyone taking part in judicial proceedings, from the judge to the witnesses. Absolute privilege extends equally to any proceedings of a judicial nature, such as those of the disciplinary bodies of the professions, eg the General Medical Council. Fair and accurate reports of judicial proceedings in the UK are similarly protected. (In some circumstances, the defence of privilege cannot be used in respect of such reports where the action relates to a 'spent' offence under the Rehabilitation of Offenders Act, 1974.)

Communications between a solicitor and his client are privileged, but there is some doubt whether the privilege is absolute or qualified. There are similar doubts about the privilege bestowed on communications in the course of duty between persons holding public office. It is possible that, in the latter case, the degree of privilege would depend upon the seniority of the officials concerned. For instance, a government minister might enjoy absolute privilege whereas a police constable might enjoy only qualified privilege.

Where someone is protected by qualified privilege, he can be successfully sued for defamation only if it is proved that he did not make the statement in question honestly. He will be liable if he was motivated by malice. Qualified privilege is granted to fair and accurate reports of parliamentary proceedings and of judicial proceedings open to the public (including foreign proceedings if of public interest in this country). (Again, this particular defence may not be available in the case of a spent offence under the Rehabilitation of Offenders Act, 1974.) It is also extended to fair and accurate reports in the press and on radio and television of certain topics of public interest; these are listed by statute and include parliamentary and judicial proceedings in some commonwealth countries, proceedings in international organisations of which this country is a member, public meetings, meetings of companies and decisions of various public bodies.

An important aspect of qualified privilege is that it applies to references given by one employer to another. Indeed, it applies where anyone is under a duty to inform another who is interested in the character of a third party. The duty need not be a legal one but it is vital to the claim of qualified privilege that there should be a moral duty which most people would recognise.

If the person making the statement is doing so to protect his own legitimate interest, he may be able to claim qualified privilege. For instance, he may be denying an allegation against himself. Again, the person to whom he communicates the statement may be under an obligation to protect his interests.

Communications between people who have a common interest in the matter discussed may be privileged, provided that such a common interest really exists.

Where a communication would otherwise not be actionable it will not become so if it is published to a third person in the ordinary course of business. The most obvious example of this is the dictation to a secretary of a letter containing statements about the person to whom it is addressed which would be defamatory were they published to a third person.

4 *Unintentional Defamation followed by an Apology.* Generally, it is no defence that defamation was unintentional. However, there is a statutory exception to this principle. If someone who publishes a statement, which he did not and should not have known to be defamatory, offers as soon as practicable to make an apology in suitable form, to try to notify everyone to whom the statement has been distributed and to pay the aggrieved party's reasonable costs, this will be a defence to an action of defamation. However, if the offer is not accepted and if the person sued is not the author of the statement, it must be shown, for the defence to succeed, that the author wrote it without malice.

Generally, an apology and offer to make amends, though not a defence, will help to reduce the amount of damages which the plaintiff will be able to recover.

5 *Vulgar Abuse.* It will be appreciated from what has been said above that if a reasonable man might be expected to believe a statement so that a person's reputation suffers or he becomes socially shunned, it would be no defence to claim that the statement was mere abuse and not meant to be taken literally. Therefore, in order to avoid liability for defamation in this way, the defendant must establish not only that the statement was merely vituperative, but that the surrounding circumstances of its publication were such that this must have been evident to the person to whom it was published. Obviously, as this is really a 'heat-of-the-moment' defence, it is more applicable to spoken than to written statements.

The Distinction between Libel and Slander

If a defamatory statement is in some permanent form, such as a book or a film, it will be libellous. It is also provided by statute that defamatory statements broadcast over radio and television are libellous. If the statement is of an ephemeral nature, such as one made in conversation, it will be slanderous. The distinction is important because anyone who is defamed by libel can sue whether or not he can show that he has suffered any material loss. If successful, he will obtain damages merely for loss of reputation, although, naturally, he can recover an additional sum for any actual damage which he has suffered. However, subject to the four exceptions mentioned below, no legal action can be brought by someone who has been slandered, unless he can show that he has suffered material damage. The exceptions are as follows:

1 An imputation that someone has committed a criminal offence punishable by imprisonment. It makes no difference if the statement alleges a past conviction, since this is just as likely to make people shun the plaintiff.

2 The imputation of a contagious disease which would prevent the plaintiff from mixing with other people.

3 An imputation that a woman is unchaste. (This would include an allegation of adultery.) In order to discourage needless lawsuits, it is provided by statute that the plaintiff cannot recover more costs than the damages which she obtains, unless the judge certifies that she had good reason to bring the action. If only nominal damages are recovered, the plaintiff will find herself out of pocket unless she recovers her costs.

4 Words calculated to disparage someone in any office, profession, calling, trade or business held or carried on by him at the time of the publication of the statement. This is the most important exception. To fall within it, it is not necessary that the statement should have referred to the way in which the plaintiff carried on his duties in the particular calling in question. It is enough if the remark, by damaging his reputation as a person, damages his reputation in his job. It is doubtful whether this exception applies to honorary offices.

10 Cars

Owning a Car

Taxing the Car

All cars must display a current excise licence which is visible from the nearside. To obtain an excise licence, the motorist applies to his local taxation office. He will have to pay a fee and also produce:

A completed application form (obtainable from any post office).

Insurance certificate.

MOT test certificate (if the car is over three years old).

The vehicle registration (log) book.

Subsequently the excise licence can be renewed at a post office provided this is done prior to the day it expires, but all the above documents must again be produced, together with the expiring licence disc.

A Driver and Vehicle Licensing Centre (DVLC) at Swansea has taken over this work from local authorities. It is compiling a central record of all drivers in Great Britain, as well as issuing driving licences and dealing with vehicle taxation.

New Registration Document

When a new car is registered, the DVLC will not issue the present vehicle registration (log) book; instead, the owner will receive a computer registration document stating:

The name of the current owner.

The date he bought (ie registered) the car.

The date the car itself was registered (ie its age).

The number of previous owners.

Log Book

The present log book gives much more information. It further identifies the vehicle by stating its make, type, colour, registration mark, and its engine and chassis numbers. If a car is repainted in a different colour, or engine capacity is increased, it is an offence not to register the change and have it officially noted in the log book.

Driving Licences

The driving licences now issued by the DVLC have to be renewed every three years. Until 1977 some drivers will still have the red booklet licence issued from a local taxation office. Eventually licences will be issued to last until the driver reaches the age of seventy, after which they will be renewable every three years. Local taxation offices will transfer a driver's records to the DVLC when he applies to have his licence renewed. Application forms for driving licences are available from local taxation offices and post offices.

Legally, the licence wallet now being issued is of special interest. When the licence is folded inside it in the normal way, any endorsements cannot be seen. A police officer examining a licence is not entitled in law to remove the licence from its wallet, and therefore has no means of knowing whether it has been endorsed.

Changes of Ownership

When a car changes hands, the seller must notify his local vehicle taxation office. Failure to do so promptly can involve a fine of up to £20. The buyer too must register (even if the car is being bought on hire purchase and is, therefore, legally owned by a finance company). Failure to send the log book to register the particulars can involve the buyer in a fine of up to £50.

Some sellers forget to notify a sale, so the taxation office writes to the previous owner as a matter of routine when the buyer seeks to register his car. The taxation office will then normally keep the registration book until it receives confirmation of the sale from the previous owner.

Buying or Selling a Car

Registration and Ownership

The importance of registration is particularly evident when vehicles are bought and sold. Anyone who offers a car for sale but cannot produce the registration book should be regarded with suspicion. This does not mean that the log book proves legal ownership of the car. It merely states who is the registered 'keeper'. For example, a car may be registered in a person's name, but in fact belong to his employers or, more commonly, to a finance company. The seller can prove he owns the car offered by producing the log book together with:

His original order form given by the dealer (if he bought it new); or

A receipt for the money he paid when he bought it; or

His consumer credit agreement, and his final receipt for the last instalment paid to the finance company.

There are two principles that buyers and sellers should observe with great care:

1 The buyer should always insist on receiving the log book immediately he hands over his money. If it is not available, he should put off paying until he does receive it; he could, for example, pay by post-dated cheque. If the log book does not arrive on the agreed date, perhaps by the first post, he could stop his cheque.

2 The seller should insist on cash or on clearing the buyer's cheque before he hands over the log book. Alternatively, he could ask the buyer to pay by banker's draft (which cannot be stopped).

This situation could result in a stalemate. If buyer and seller are so distrustful of each other that even agreeing a common date for the exchange of money and log book is unacceptable, then their best course is not to proceed at all but to go instead to a reputable dealer.

Secondhand Cars

Where the mileometer gives a false reading, suggesting that the car has done less mileage than it really has, the dealer is liable to be fined, even though he was not dishonest, did not interfere with the mileometer, had no knowledge of the falsity of its reading, or the purchaser was not really interested in whether it was right or wrong.

A person who sells a secondhand car will be well advised to disclaim any responsibility for the accuracy of the mileometer, and to point out to the buyer the possibility that the mileage it shows may be wrong.

The Condition of the Car

Nowadays it is very dangerous for the seller to exaggerate the quality of his wares (see also Chapter 14). A dealer was recently prosecuted for describing a secondhand car as a 'beautiful model', when in fact though it looked very fine the engine was unsound. The court held that by describing the car as 'beautiful' the dealer was assuring the buyer that its mechanical condition was also good. He was convicted of an offence under the Trade Descriptions Act, 1968, and was duly fined.

Dealer's Liability

The law requires a higher degree of expert knowledge from a dealer than from an ordinary private seller. A dealer who misleads a car owner about the condition and hence the trade-in value of his car, and persuades him to accept an unfairly low price, can be committing an offence, and would also be liable to pay the seller the car's true value.

Whilst a private seller of a car cannot be prosecuted under the Trade Descriptions Act he could be made to pay the buyer damages under the Misrepresentation Act, 1967, for any incorrect statement that he may make. For example, he may tell a prospective buyer that the car is a 'good runner'. This will, in law, mean that it is mechanically well maintained. If an inherent defect then becomes apparent, the seller could not avoid paying damages unless he could prove that he had reasonable grounds for believing that the car was well-maintained (eg it had just been thoroughly overhauled).

Sale of Unroadworthy Vehicles

Under the Road Traffic Act, 1972, it is an offence to sell a vehicle in an unroadworthy condition; this covers brakes, steering, lights and tyres.

To avoid conviction, the seller would have to prove that he had good reason to believe that the car would not be used in that condition. He should write out a list of defects and get the buyer to sign and insist on his written undertaking not to use the car until those defects are repaired.

Buying from a Dealer

Before 1973 the manufacturer's guarantee was expressed to be in substitution for all other legal rights given by statute or common law. Now, whether the car is new or secondhand, the law gives the buyer a guarantee which the seller's 'small-print' exclusion clauses cannot take away. Today, any guarantee given by the seller or manufacturer can only add to the rights given to the buyer by law. These rights are that:

The car should be of 'merchantable quality'—which basically means it must be reasonably fit for use as a motor car.

It must be truthfully described, eg 'one owner', or '1970 model', etc.

It must be fit for any special purpose promised by the seller, eg the buyer may ask and be told that the car is 'suitable for rough farm roads'.

If a new car breaks down due to some defect, it must be repaired entirely free of charge by the dealer. He cannot charge for labour and he must also provide another car for the buyer to use while it is off the road, or reimburse him if he has to hire one.

Certificate of Examination

Naturally, in the case of a secondhand car, any defects pointed out to the buyer before he buys cannot be complained of later. Nor, if the buyer examines the car, can he later complain of obvious defects he ought to have seen. To forestall such complaints, some car dealers now insist the buyer signs a 'certificate of examination'. By signing, the buyer will acknowledge he has inspected the car. As this will very largely prevent him claiming later for defects that he ought to have seen, he will be better off if he refuses to sign or, better still, insists that the seller lists the defects on the certificate, which both then sign. Alternatively, the buyer should employ an engineer to inspect the car and give a full report (eg through the AA). If a serious hidden defect later emerges which is not on the report, the buyer could still reject the car as not 'merchantable'.

Insuring a Car

Minimum Cover

It is a serious offence for an owner to use a car or permit anyone to use his car without third-party insurance. If convicted, he would be liable to a fine of up to £200. His licence would almost invariably be endorsed, and he could also be disqualified from driving for a period.

The policy of insurance must cover any claim in respect of death or injury to any person arising out of the use of the vehicle on a road. This now includes any passenger riding in the policy-holder's car who may be injured. It also covers the emergency treatment of anyone injured, but it does not have to cover damage to another vehicle or to property, eg if the car is driven into someone's house (although, in practice, all policies invariably cover damage to property, and to other cars as well).

Comprehensive Insurance

Most drivers will prefer wider insurance cover than the legal minimum. Comprehensive cover will ensure that the car is replaced or repaired if it is damaged or written off in an accident due to the policy-holder's own negligence. Also, limited personal-accident benefits are usually given under most comprehensive policies if the driver is killed or disabled through his own bad driving. On the other hand, if a passenger travels in a car not knowing that the driver has no insurance cover, he would not be committing an offence in this particular instance.

Special Protection for Employees

There is only one exception to the absolute prohibition on driving without insurance. An employee driving one of his firm's vehicles on the firm's business commits no offence, provided he is not aware that the firm has no insurance covering him to drive. But the firm could be convicted for permitting an employee to drive while uninsured.

Social and Business Purposes

Where the policy restricts the use of the car to social, domestic and pleasure purposes, the policy-holder would be driving without insurance if he went on a business trip. But if he gave a lift out of courtesy to a friend who was on a business round, this would be regarded as social. This applies also to carrying a friend for a pleasure trip; even though the friend pays for his petrol, this still counts as a social use. But if the policy-holder himself took on passengers who paid for their petrol, this would amount to 'hire or reward', and he would be uninsured unless his policy covered it. If, too, the car is insured for business and the policy specifies one particular business, the policy-holder would not be covered if he used it for a different business.

Lending the Car

The policy may cover any person driving with the policy-holder's permission, provided he holds or has held a driving licence and is not disqualified. It would still be operative even if his licence had expired and he had forgotten to renew it. It will also cover a friend who holds an international or foreign licence (providing he has been here for less than one year) unless the policy specifically excluded foreign licence holders. A learner driver would also be covered, although he would only have a provisional licence.

The Motor Insurers' Bureau

Anyone injured by a hit-and-run driver who could not be traced, or by a driver who had broken the law by having no insurance cover, would be unable to make an insurance claim in the normal way. Although in the latter case the driver might go to prison, the person injured would have little chance of getting damages from him.

To meet this kind of situation, the Motor Insurers' Bureau was set up by Parliament in 1946. It will pay those injured the full damages ordered by the court, even though the uninsured driver is unable to pay them. Since 1969 it will also compensate the hit-and-run victim where the driver is unknown and so cannot be sued. But the injured person must file a claim within three years.

Compensation by the Bureau may, however, not be total. A brand new car, worth several thousand pounds, may be hit by an uninsured driver: the car turns out to be a complete write-off but the owner himself only suffers bruises. The Motor Insurers' Bureau will pay him for personal injury, say £50, but not for the value of the car. If the uninsured driver is penniless, he will in fact get nothing for the car since only comprehensive insurance cover will meet this situation.

How to Keep a No-claim Bonus

After an accident the policy-holder's own insurance company will usually pay his claim even though the other driver was wholly to blame. This is because most companies have a 'knock for knock' agreement. To ensure his no-claim bonus will not be affected, a driver should make it clear when notifying his insurers that he was in no way responsible for the accident. All reputable companies will accept this and leave the no-claim bonus intact. If this does not happen, the policy-holder can claim from the other driver. Similarly, if he has, say, a £25 excess under his policy, he can insist that the other driver also pays this as well as the cost of hiring a substitute car while his own is being repaired. The other driver's insurance company will normally pay these items if it is satisfied that he was to blame.

Duty to Report an Accident

Motorists are under a duty to stop and exchange particulars when they are involved in an accident in which damage has occurred to either motor vehicle. If names and addresses are not exchanged then the motorist must report the accident to the police as soon as possible and, in any case, within twenty-four hours.

If personal injury has occurred, names and addresses must be exchanged and the police must be informed unless the motorist has produced his certificate of insurance at the scene of the accident.

The law has now been extended so that accidents involving damage to traffic signs, bollards or anything attached to the highway must be reported to the police.

Driving and the Law

The best guide to good driving is the Highway Code. If a motorist has failed to observe a provision of the Highway Code, his failure can be put forward in court by the prosecution as proof of his bad driving.

Types of Offence

Bad driving is chiefly classified under the Road Traffic Act, 1972, as either careless or dangerous. A charge of careless driving is the less serious, and can only be tried by a magistrates' court. A motorist also charged with dangerous driving would have the right to ask for his case to be tried by a jury at a crown court. Conviction at the crown court might carry a higher penalty. If he is acquitted at the crown court of dangerous driving, a motorist may still be summoned back to the magistrates' court to face the charge of careless driving.

A motorist who admits that his driving was reprehensible will often ask for both charges to be dealt with by the magistrates. His lawyer may be able to persuade the court and the prosecution to drop the more serious charge.

Illness While Driving

A motorist who falls asleep at the wheel and goes to the wrong side of the road or hits the pavement would be guilty of careless driving (and possibly dangerous driving too) because he should have stopped when he began to feel sleepy. But if he loses control through a sudden, unexpected illness, he should be found not guilty, unless he knows he is subject to dizzy spells or blackouts.

Sudden Loss of Control

A motorist who finds himself unexpectedly blinded by headlights, or who for any other reason cannot control his car, should stop at once. For example, a dog travelling in the car may jump unexpectedly on to his lap, or he may be hit by a stone, or an insect may get into his eye. If he does not stop his car immediately, he will be liable for any ensuing bad driving.

Convictions Leading to Disqualification

A conviction either for careless or dangerous driving can carry a sentence of disqualification. In fact disqualification would be rare on a first offence, which would be noted by endorsement on the driver's licence. This is a first step towards disqualification. If a driver has two previous endorsements in the last three years, the magistrates will normally disqualify him for at least six months.

Anyone convicted of dangerous driving twice within three years must be disqualified for at least twelve months, unless there are 'special reasons' (see p 129). It is also important to remember that the three-year period runs from the date of the first conviction to the date of the second offence, not from conviction to conviction. A driver cannot avoid the three-year period by getting the hearing of his second case postponed.

Disqualification from driving applies to any sort of vehicle. Any attempt to drive a vehicle while disqualified can carry a prison sentence. It is unwise to drive to court if there is a possibility that one may be disqualified, because the ban on driving is immediate.

Getting the Licence Back

The court has the power to remove a disqualification after a certain lapse of time. A driver cannot apply to have his licence back until at least two years have passed. Anyone disqualified for more than four years must serve a full half of the period before he can apply, while a driver disqualified for more than ten years must wait five years before applying.

Compulsory Endorsement, with or without Disqualification

Even on a first offence of dangerous driving, there is a risk of disqualification. Disqualification is also possible for a variety of lesser offences, among them:

Careless driving.

Failing to stop after an accident.

Driving while uninsured.

Failing to comply with traffic signals.

Leaving a car in a dangerous position.

Driving while disqualified (although further disqualification is no longer obligatory).

In all these cases the magistrates must endorse the driver's licence, unless there are special reasons. They do not have to disqualify him unless the case is one of exceptional gravity.

Compulsory Disqualification

Besides any other penalty that the court may impose, it is obliged in the absence of special reasons to disqualify the motorist for at least one year if he is convicted of:

Causing death by dangerous driving.

Driving while unfit through drink or drugs.

Driving with excess alcohol in the blood (over 80mg of alcohol per 100ml of blood).

Refusing to provide a blood or urine specimen.

A second 'drink' conviction within ten years carries an automatic three-year disqualification.

Avoiding Disqualification or Endorsement

Provided there are 'special reasons' the court is not obliged to order disqualification or endorsement.

The meaning of 'special reasons' is highly technical and very restricted. A special reason must relate to the circumstances of the offence, eg its comparative triviality. A circumstance relating to the driver himself, eg that he was disabled or that driving was vital to his work, is not a special reason.

A motorist who, at a party, thought he was drinking lemonade when in fact someone had 'laced' his drink with gin would have a special reason to avoid disqualification.

The fact that a doctor, for example, might lose his livelihood if disqualified would *not* amount to a special reason. Nor would it in the case of an invalid totally dependent on his car. This kind of personal plea would not help on a drink conviction but might constitute *mitigating circumstances* which would entitle a court to refrain from disqualifying a driver who is subject to 'totting up', ie who has two minor disqualifiable offences endorsed on his licence during the previous three years. His good character, the hardship he might suffer through losing his licence, the fact that the third offence was not in itself serious, might all help him to avoid disqualification despite the totting-up rule.

Seat Belts

All new cars must be fitted with seat belts. A passenger who omits to wear a seat belt could forfeit part of his right to compensation in the event of an accident. If, for example, a passenger is injured in an accident and successfully sues the driver, the damages he receives will be substantially reduced if it can be shown that he contributed to his own injuries by failing to wear a seat belt.

Parking

Where to Park

One of the most difficult problems facing the car owner is knowing where he may park free of the threat of prosecution. Generally, in a town, there are three solutions:

In an official car park.

At a parking meter.

On a broken yellow line (but only during the hours permitted on the official notices).

Parking is also tacitly permitted on minor roads in towns provided no obstruction is caused.

When parked, the car must be at least fifteen yards from any road junction, facing in the same direction as the traffic on that side of the road, and as close to the kerb as possible. Even if he obeys all these regulations, a driver can still be prosecuted if his car causes an unnecessary obstruction. Car lights need not be left on when parking within the 30mph speed-limit signs, but lorries, coaches and trailers must show lights wherever they park.

Drivers should also remember that they may not stop:

On a rural clearway, except at an official lay-by.

On a motorway, except in emergency, and then only on the hard shoulder.

Motorists parking in such a way as to be a danger to other people using the road are liable to disqualification or licence endorsement. Offences in this category include leaving the car on a blind corner, or on a slope with the hand-brake off. Stopping within the limits of a pedestrian crossing carries an automatic endorsement.

Anyone opening a car door in such a way as to cause danger or injury is liable to a fine.

Yellow Lines

The significance of the yellow lines is clearly set out in the Highway Code, except in one important respect. Unfortunately, the Highway

Code gives the impression that a single yellow line prohibits parking on working days only, and that motorists are free to park there for any length of time on a Sunday. This is not so.

Loading

On some roads it is only permitted to park for the purposes of loading or unloading. This excludes shopping but not stopping to pick up items already purchased. An obstruction may be wilful or 'unnecessary'.

When does a parked car become an 'unnecessary' obstruction, so that leaving it in such a position amounts to an offence? The length of time is the deciding factor. The police must show that the parking was an unreasonable use of the road, either because of its duration, eg several hours, or because of the place, eg near a junction. On the other hand, it is not unreasonable for a milk float to stop occasionally to sell milk. Nor is it unreasonable for a driver to stop his car because of a breakdown, provided he takes steps to remove it as soon as possible.

The police do not need to prove that anyone was actually obstructed, since the mere presence of the car means that that part of the road is potentially blocked to other users.

Private householders are often troubled by motorists parking outside their property, but they cannot stop a motorist parking on the highway. Nevertheless, the longer a car remains there the more likely the police are to consider the vehicle an unnecessary obstruction.

Lines of Defence

It is no defence to a charge of unnecessary obstruction that a vehicle was only one of a line of vehicles already parked. The only defence to this charge is to show that the obstruction was vital. A reasonable example might be the case of a doctor parking for an emergency visit.

Summary

Motorists have no right to park (as distinct from stopping to pick up or set down passengers or for loading) unless there is a parking meter or a notice that parking is permitted. Anyone in doubt should ask a traffic warden or a policeman, whose approval would mean that the motorist would be safe from prosecution at least until another warden or policeman came along and told him to move.

The fact that there are notices restricting parking during certain hours does not give the motorist an absolute right to park outside restricted hours.

The owner or hirer of a vehicle which incurs a parking penalty can be compelled to pay it, even though he can prove that he was not driving it at the time of the offence.

Where Not to Drive

There are also restrictions as to where a car may be driven. For example:

Under the Highways Act, 1835, it is an offence to drive on the footway.

Under the Road Traffic Act, 1972, it is an offence to drive on footpaths or on any land which is not part of a road. Offences against this part of the Act carry a maximum penalty of £10.

If You Are Stopped by the Police

You should pull over and stop as soon as any officer in uniform or a marked police car signals you to do so. Your conduct may in practice greatly influence the actions of the police officer, but this is outside the scope of this book. However, it is wise not to apologise, as this could be taken as implying guilt. Do not enter into any argument with a police officer. You are not legally obliged to answer his questions, and in practice you would be ill-advised to discuss the incident, since the officer is likely to make a note of your remarks and recite them in court. Give him your name and address and date of birth, and if pressed further, say 'I am not prepared to enter into a discussion'.

Production of Documents

The officer will ask you to produce:

Your driving licence.

An insurance certificate.

An MOT test certificate.

You may not have these documents with you, in which case the police officer will hand you a form requiring you to produce them at any police station in the UK within five days.

When you show him your licence he is not entitled to look at the back pages (or to remove the new-style green licence from its plastic wallet) to see if you have any convictions.

You are not obliged to make a statement to the police, nor are you obliged to accompany the officer to the station. But in certain circumstances he may say he is arresting you, in which case you should not resist.

When You May Be Arrested

The officer has the power to arrest you:

If your breath test shows positive (green).

If you refuse a breath test.

If you are disqualified from driving.

If you obstruct the highway. (Rarely enforced unless you are awkward.)

If you are guilty of careless or dangerous driving and he suspects you have given a false name and address, or if you refuse to give him any particulars at all.

When Must the Police Serve on a Motorist Notice of Intended Prosecution?

Where no accident has occurred, you cannot normally be convicted of certain offences, in particular speeding, dangerous or careless driving, disobeying a traffic sign or signal (including double white lines) or leaving your car in a dangerous position, *unless*:

The officer warned you at the time that you might be prosecuted, or

You receive a notice of intended prosecution within fourteen days.

On the other hand, receiving such a notice does not mean that the police will prosecute, only that they may do so.

11 Business Law

Starting a Business

An initial choice for anyone who goes into any business is the legal form which the business will take. The simplest course is for the business to be owned personally by the businessman. The assets and liabilities of the firm will be legally indistinguishable from those of the proprietor. This is so even if the firm trades under another name. The other options are to form a partnership with one or more other persons, or to form a company.

Partnership

The obvious advantage of forming a partnership is that each partner can contribute skills, time or capital to the common enterprise.

However, in a full partnership, each partner is liable for the liabilities of the firm, not only to the extent of his share in the firm but also to the extent of all his personal assets. This is so whether the debts are incurred by himself or by his partners. The principle applies not only to trade debts but to other obligations, such as negligence or fraud by one of the partners. Consequently, if the firm is unable to meet its obligations the creditors can, if necessary, bankrupt all the partners in order to obtain payment.

Limited Partnership

There is a way in which a partner who has put up capital but does not take part in running the business can be protected against this risk. The partnership articles can provide that such a partner is liable only up to the amount of his share. This 'limited partnership' must be registered at the Companies' Registry.

It has been possible to form a limited partnership since 1907 but until recently little use has been made of this facility. Generally, it was preferred to form private limited liability companies. However, since 1967 such companies have had to make public their accounts. Limited partnerships are therefore now the only way in which limited liability can be combined with financial secrecy.

A limited partnership, unlike other partnerships, must be in writing.

Terms of the Partnership

The relations between the partners are laid down by the Partnership Act, 1890, unless there is an agreement stipulating a different arrangement. Thus, where no specific period is agreed for the duration of the partnership it is called a partnership 'at will', and any partner may end it at any time by giving to the others notice of termination. This notice is best given in writing and a separate notice should be sent to each customer also.

Customers who receive no notice of one partner's withdrawal are entitled to assume he is still engaged in the business and to hold him liable. He should ensure, therefore, that his name is taken off all letter and bill headings. If the business seems to be heading for disaster, the safest way of notifying new customers of his disassociation is by advertisement in a newspaper, in particular in the *London Gazette*.

Until a customer has notice of a partner's withdrawal, that partner will continue to be responsible for anything that his fellow partners do in the normal course of the firm's business. This responsibility can be quite extensive. In a trading partnership, for example, where the business is based on buying and selling goods, outsiders are entitled to assume that each of the partners has authority to borrow money and to pledge the firm's goods as security for borrowing. They can also assume that he has authority to draw and endorse cheques and for a host of other acts necessary for purposes of credit. It will be no protection to the other partners if the partnership agreement in fact prohibited any partner from committing the firm in the way in question. If the person dealing with the partnership was unaware of this restriction and if he was entitled to assume that the partner had authority, the firm will be bound.

During the partnership, each partner has certain rights unless the contrary is agreed. Each partner has free access to the firm's books, and when examining them he may employ an accountant or any 'unobjectionable' agent to assist him. Normally, where a partnership is for a fixed period, a partner cannot be expelled unless the other partners have an express power of expulsion, written into the partnership agreement. Similarly, the firm may not take a new partner without the consent of all partners, nor may they change the nature of the partnership business without the consent of every partner.

Before entering into a partnership agreement it is important to have the help and advice of a solicitor or accountant in drawing up an agreement which will specify such matters as:

Sharing profits, and responsibility for debts.

The duration of the partnership.

The length of notice each partner must give to dissolve the partnership.

Voting rights. Each partner normally has equal voting rights, but the partnership agreement may give the senior partner the power of veto, or it may give certain partners double voting rights.

Other business interest. No partner may engage in any activity which competes with the partnership business, but he is otherwise free to engage in other business interests unless the agreement prohibits this.

It is possible to include in the partnership agreement a provision expressly forbidding a partner starting up in competition after leaving. This prohibition must not be wider than is absolutely necessary to give reasonable protection to the firm's business. If it goes too far it will be unenforceable.

Forming a Limited Company

A sole trader may protect himself by registering as a limited company. A limited company is a means by which he can carry on his business without the risk of going bankrupt and losing his personal assets. If the company cannot meet all its debts, all he will lose when it goes into liquidation is the money he has put into it as capital.

Only two shareholders are needed, for example the trader and his wife. Partners may also be better off operating as a limited company if they are in a speculative business.

Disadvantages

One disadvantage of a limited company is the loss of secrecy since it must file its accounts every year with the Registrar of Companies. Any member of the public is entitled to go to the Companies' Registry and see what the company earns. The object is to allow the public and other traders and suppliers to decide whether the company is credit-worthy.

How to Form a Limited Company

A number of firms will form a standard type of company relatively cheaply and speedily. If you want a tailor-made company and also the opportunity of general legal advice you should approach a solicitor, but be prepared to pay considerably more.

The documents required to register a company are complicated. The two most important are:

The memorandum of association, which defines the scope and nature of the company's business. Its trading powers may be limited to a particular trade, but often will cover a variety of business enterprises to allow for expansion.

The articles of association, which deal with the way the company is run internally.

The name of the company may not be similar to an existing company or suggest that business is being carried on a larger scale than is in fact the case. It must always be followed with the word 'limited'. All business and other document letters must state the name of the company, its registration number and place of registration. This is so even if the company trades under a different 'business name' which is also shown. Unless exemption is obtained the names of all directors must also be shown on all letters, trade circulars and similar documents. The company's name must be displayed outside its registered office.

A limited company differs from a partnership in several ways:

Limited Company	**Partnership**
A limited company is a legal entity, quite apart from its members. It can own property and assets in its own right.	The partnership has no legal personality of its own, although the partners often refer to themselves as John Smith & Company.
A limited company has the advantage of continuous existence.	The assets of a partnership must be held by trustees or the partners jointly.

Limited Company	Partnership
The death or bankruptcy of one or all of its members has no effect on its existence.	The death or bankruptcy of a partner brings about the dissolution of the partnership.
The liability of members is limited to the amount unpaid on their shares.	The liability of partners is unlimited except in the case of a limited partnership where the limited partners only can escape full liability for business debts in the event of insolvency. The other partners are fully liable even to the extent of their personal assets.
The company can be formed only by the process of registration which is complicated and expensive.	A partnership (except a limited partnership) can be formed without formality, eg by word of mouth or simply by the fact of going into business together, although a written agreement or deed of partnership is highly desirable.
The shares are freely transferable in the case of a public company (although a private company places restrictions on the transfer of its shares, eg they may not be sold without the consent of the directors).	No partner may transfer his shares without the consent of the other partners.

Unlimited Companies

Once a private company is established in business the danger of it failing may be very slight. If it wishes, it can re-register as an unlimited company, and (provided it does not own and is not owned by a limited company) so avoid having to annex its accounts and auditors' reports and director's report to its annual return at Companies House. It can thus secure greater privacy, providing its members are willing to forego the advantage of limited liability in the event of the business failing.

In most other respects the unlimited company has the same attributes as the limited company. Although the liability of each member is unlimited, it is restricted to his share of the company's debt. In the event of liquidation, a past member is liable only if he has ceased to be a member within one year of winding up.

Since 1967 many private limited companies with no fear of insolvency have dispensed with limited liability to obtain the advantage of secrecy. The directors are also no longer obliged to file information about subsidiary companies or political contributions.

An unlimited company can re-register as a limited company; but no company can change its nature more than once.

The Business Name

Whatever the form of a business, it can trade under a name different from the name or names of the proprietors or of the company. However, it must first register the chosen name with the Registrar of Business Names. The registrar has power to refuse to register a name if, for example, it is likely to be confused with an existing name. After registration, any changes in ownership of the business must be notified to the registrar. There are penalties for failure to observe these requirements.

There is no way in which someone can be prevented from trading under his own name, even if this happens to be identical with that of an established competitor.

12 Employment Law

The Employer/Employee Relationship

Contracts of Employment

It may not seem a very difficult problem to decide whether one person is employing another, in other words whether a contract of employment exists between them. In most offices, shops or factories this will be clear enough. However, in many cases the courts have had to decide this question and to try to define what constitutes a contract of employment. This can be of great practical importance in determining the parties' rights.

Traditionally, the test for distinguishing between a 'contract of service' (employer/employee) and a 'contract for services' (independent contractors) has been that in the former the employer retains control over the way in which the employee performs his duties. However, this is by no means always a helpful test, particularly where the employer can exercise little or no control because he lacks the requisite expertise. A satisfactory modern definition of a contract of employment has yet to be evolved.

Status of Civil Servants

It is not always appreciated that established civil servants hold their appointments at the pleasure of the Crown and in most cases are not regarded by the law as having a contract of employment. However, in some cases special provisions are made for them by statute, as in the case of redundancy payments.

Employees of national corporations such as the BBC or the Bank of England are not civil servants. Police officers are (legally) neither servants of the Crown nor of the police authority. (They are, however, treated as the authority's employees for the purposes of 'vicarious liability'—see p 141).

The Duties of an Employer

An employer is under a duty to take reasonable care for the health, safety and welfare at work of all his employees. Some of his obligations are imposed on him by the common law, others by statute.

Statutory Regulations

There are a great number of detailed statutory regulations, eg Factory Acts, 1961, Offices, Shops & Railway Premises Act, 1963. These range from the fencing of machinery to the provision of washroom facilities, the maintenance of a minimum temperature to the amount of floor-space per office worker. It is beyond the scope of this chapter to attempt to detail them. However, subject to what has been said, they may be regarded as elaborations of the basic duty. This is commonly divided into four parts, and requires the provision of:

Competent fellow employees.

Safe plant and machinery.

A safe place of work and access to it.

A safe system of work.

If it is shown that the employer has failed to provide one or more of these requirements when it would have been reasonable to do so, he will be held to have been negligent. If he has further failed to comply with, eg the Factories Act, he is in breach of his statutory duty. If an employee establishes one or both of these grounds he is entitled to be compensated if he suffers injury.

Fellow Employees

An employer may be liable to one employee who has suffered through the action of another employee. In many cases his liability will be covered by the principle of 'vicarious liability'. He may also be liable in instances where he might have a defence under that principle, as where the fellow employee was not acting in the course of his employment: eg continuing to employ a man addicted to horseplay who by such an act injures a fellow workman. Here the employer had failed to provide competent fellow employees.

The employer's liability is a personal one and an employer may also be liable for the acts of an independent contractor, which is again outside the usual rules of vicarious liability. However, the law is not entirely clear in this respect. Note also that an employer must instruct his employees adequately, eg in use of machinery.

Safe Plant and Machinery

An employer must ensure that care is taken to supply safe equipment to his employees. He is also liable for injury caused to an employee in the course of employment as a result of defective equipment provided by the employer if the defect is wholly or partly the fault of the manufacturers of the equipment. The employer himself is entitled to recover from the manufacturer any loss which he may suffer as a result of this rule.

Safe Place of Work and Access to It

The duty to provide a safe place of work must obviously be tempered by the nature of the work. The place of employment should be as safe as the exercise of reasonable skill and care permits. A spiderman can hardly expect the same degree of security as a white-collar worker. On the other hand, it is no defence for the employer to show that the employee knew of the danger. The question is: could the danger have been eliminated or reduced? This duty also embraces situations where although the place of work was safe in construction it has become unsafe—through, as an example, oil on the floor. The test is the same.

Safe System of Work

A safe system of work must be established by the employer. He must also maintain adequate supervision to ensure that the system is observed. The degree of supervision required will be a test of reasonableness in each case. It is not essential for an employee who claims that a system is unsafe to suggest an alternative, but if the system is one that is normally used it will be hard to prove a breach of the employer's duty. Nevertheless, it will not always be enough for the employer to defend himself by saying that he had observed the relevant statutory regulations.

In industrial injury claims, the principles of 'contributory negligence' will often be relevant (see also Chapter 1).

Terms of Employment

Within thirteen weeks of the start of employment, the employer is legally bound to give his employee a written notice specifying the date his employment began and details of the following:

1 The scale or rate of pay or the method of calculating it.

2 If payment is weekly, monthly or at some other interval.

3 Terms and conditions of hours of work (including terms and conditions relating to normal working hours).

4 Any terms and conditions relating to (i) entitlement to holidays (including public holidays) and holiday pay (including accrued holiday pay on termination of employment); (ii) incapacity for work due to sickness or injury, including provision for sick pay; and (iii) pensions.

5 Length of notice to be given by employer or employee.

6 If the term of employment is fixed, the date of expiry.

7 The employee's job title.

8 Details of any disciplinary rules and of any grievance procedure, including details of a person to whom an employee should apply and of an appeals procedure.

9 Any previous employment which counts as part of the employee's continuous employment.

Such a notice need not be given to employees who work for less than sixteen hours per week. Also, if the employee has a written contract of employment setting out the relevant information there is no need for a notice.

Terminating Employment

The law lays down some minimum rights of both employer and employee to notice of termination of employment. These will normally apply unless the parties agree to terms which go beyond the legal minima. Nevertheless, there may sometimes be a longer period implied by law. For example, domestic servants are customarily entitled to four weeks' notice.

Contracts of employment for fixed terms of over four weeks are not affected nor (subject to certain exceptions) are jobs where the employee works for under sixteen hours per week. A few special categories of employee, such as registered dockers and merchant seamen, are likewise unaffected.

Minimum Periods of Notice

The minimum notice to which an employee is entitled (unless justifiably dismissed for misconduct) depends upon the length of his employment with the employer in question. This is shown on the following table:

Length of employment	*Period of notice*
4 weeks to 2 years	1 week
2 years to 12 years	1 week for each year
Over 12 years	Not less than 12 weeks

An employee must in all cases give 1 week's notice to his employer.

The period of employment must be continuous. However, for this purpose, any absences of up to twenty-six weeks at a time which are caused by illness count as part of the period of employment. Time spent in the Armed Forces does not break the continuity of the period, although it does not count towards it. Similarly, any week during which the employee was away from work as a result of a strike or lock-out does not break continuity but is not generally to be taken into account in calculating the period. In some circumstances, periods of employment of up to twenty-six weeks where the employee has worked between eight and sixteen hours a week can be included in calculating the period of his employment.

The employee always has the option to accept wages for the relevant period in lieu of notice.

Redundancy Payments

An employee who is dismissed as redundant is entitled to apply to an industrial tribunal for compensation from his employer. A 'dismissal' in this context includes a refusal by the employer to renew a fixed-term contract of employment when it expires. It also covers cases where the employee is justified in leaving because of the employer's conduct (such as non-payment of wages or, perhaps, demotion).

An employee can also claim redundancy pay if he leaves his employment, after giving due notice, following a period of lay-off or short-time working of four consecutive weeks or of any six weeks out of thirteen, unless there is reason to believe that full employment will be restored within four weeks. The amount which the employee can claim depends on his age and his length of service with the employer, as shown in the following table:

For each year of employment between ages	*Employee receives*
18 and 21	Half a week's pay
21 and 40	1 week's pay
40 and 65 (men)	$1\frac{1}{2}$ weeks' pay
40 and 60 (women)	$1\frac{1}{2}$ weeks' pay

The employee must have been employed for at least two years. The maximum week's pay for this purpose is £80 and the maximum number of years which can be counted is twenty. The week's pay for the calculation is taken as the amount which would be paid to the employee for a week worked at normal hours (excluding overtime) at the rates of pay in force immediately before the redundancy date. Men over 65 and women over 60 are not entitled to redundancy pay.

Proving Redundancy

It is vital to the employee's claim that he was dismissed by reason of redundancy. If the employer can prove that he dismissed the employee for any other reason, there will be no entitlement. The burden of proof is, however, on the employer, as it is presumed until the contrary is shown that the reason for dismissal was redundancy.

The dismissal will be treated as being by reason of redundancy if the employer has ceased, or intends to cease, to carry on the business for the purposes of which the employee was employed by him, or has ceased, or intends to cease, to carry on that business in the place where the employee was employed. The dismissal is also by reason of redundancy if the requirements of the business for employees to carry out work of a particular kind (or to carry it out in the same place) have ceased or diminished or are expected to do so.

Suitable Alternative Work

If the employer makes a written offer of suitable alternative employment which his employee unreasonably rejects, he will not have to make a redundancy payment. There is often room for dispute as to whether the alternative employment is really suitable.

Procedure for Claims

It is most important that an employee should observe the procedural requirements. Failure to do so may result in the failure of his claim. The basic rule is that within six months of the dismissal the employee must either have agreed and received the payment, or have made a claim to the employer in writing, or have referred the question of his entitlement to an industrial tribunal. The dismissal date will usually mean the date on which the employer's notice of termination expires, or when a fixed-term contract comes to an end. If the employer gives no notice, the dismissal date is the date on which termination takes effect.

The above rules will not always apply. For example, if the employer gives his employee notice and, before the notice expires, the employee himself gives written notice to terminate the employment at an earlier date, then that earlier date will be the dismissal date. This may well happen if the employee finds a new job quickly and wants to start it. The employer can then serve a counter-notice stating that if the employee does not work out his original notice the claim for redundancy pay will be contested. Even if this happens, the industrial tribunal may still allow the claim if it considers the employee's actions justifiable.

When a claim is being made where there has been a lay-off or short-time working, a written notice must be made within four weeks of the end of the lay-off or short-time period.

Unfair Dismissal

If an employee who has been in his job for at least twenty-six weeks ending with the effective date of termination, ie end of notice, considers that he has been unfairly dismissed, he can apply to an industrial tribunal for compensation from his employer.

If an employee has been dismissed it may either be by reason of redundancy (see above) or he may have been unfairly dismissed. In either event a claim can be made to an industrial tribunal. Claims are made on a form which can be obtained from the Department of Employment. If an employee is unsure whether his dismissal is for redundancy or an unfair dismissal, he does not have to elect but can let the tribunal decide: it is for the employer and not the employee to show that the dismissal was fair.

In order to claim for unfair dismissal an employee must have been in the employment for twenty-six weeks ending with the effective date of termination of his employment (that is, the expiry of the notice of dismissal). The claim must be made to the tribunal within three months.

There are certain classes of employment which are outside the 'unfair dismissal' provisions. These include undertakings with less than four employees, part-time workers, registered dock workers and crews of fishing vessels.

If the employee has reached 65 (or if she is a woman 60) before the effective termination of the employment, no claim can be made.

Once the claim has been made it is for the employer to show the reason (or if there were more than one the principal reason) for dismissal. He must show that:

(i) the reason for the dismissal related to the capability or qualifications of the employee for performing his job; or
(ii) related to the employee's conduct; or
(iii) was that the employee was redundant; or
(iv) was that the employee could not continue to work in the position which he held without contravention (either on his part or on that of his employer) of a statutory duty or restriction.

If the employer establishes one of the above reasons, or other substantial cause for dismissal, it still has to be established whether the dismissal was fair or unfair. To prove that it was fair, the employer will have to satisfy the industrial tribunal that, in the legal phrase, 'having regard to equity and the substantial merits of the case', he acted reasonably in treating that particular ground as a sufficient reason for dismissing the employee. What is reasonable is a question for the tribunal, but in this context it is important to note that the statutory Code of Practice in force is often relevant. Although failure to observe the provisions of the Code of Practice does not render an employer liable to any proceedings, it is admissible in evidence before the tribunal and any such failure can be taken into account in deciding whether the dismissal was fair or unfair. For example, the Code of Practice lays down a system of warnings. An employee should be warned at least twice that he is in danger of dismissal and at least one of these warnings must be in writing. For instance, if an employee is not performing his work adequately, this is in itself a good reason for dismissal (as stated above). However, it is not sufficient for the employer to show that the employee was not carrying out his work adequately if the employee had not received the appropriate warnings, had not been told in what respects he was required to improve his performance and had not been given an opportunity to do so.

If the employer states that the principal reason for the employee's dismissal was redundancy, he still has to show that the employee was not unfairly selected for redundancy. For example, other employees holding the same post may not have been dismissed and it must be shown that the established procedure in such cases has been followed.

The Trade Union and Labour Relations Act, 1974, contains very important provisions relating to dismissal for reasons related to trade union activity. However, these are outside the scope of this book.

If the tribunal finds that the employee has been unfairly dismissed, it can order that he should be re-employed. If the employer refuses to co-operate, the employee can be awarded extra compensation of up to £4,160. In any event the employee will be entitled to a 'basic award' which is calculated in almost the same way as a redundancy payment. In addition he is entitled to a 'compensatory award' based on the loss to the employee in so far as it is attributable to the action of the employer.

The usual matters which are the subject of compensation are loss of earnings (after deduction of any unemployment benefit), travelling expenses in obtaining new employment, and holiday pay. Other factors that might be taken into account are loss of the employee's right not to be unfairly dismissed (usually a compensation for this would be fairly nominal), luncheon vouchers, employer's pension contributions, etc. The maximum compensation award is £5,200.

The award can be reduced if the tribunal considers that the employee contributed to or caused acts leading to his dismissal or if the employee refuses an offer of reinstatement. The employee is under the usual duty to 'mitigate his loss' by finding new employment as soon as practicable.

Wrongful Dismissal

Whereas the right to compensation for 'unfair dismissal' is a statutory right introduced by the Industrial Relations Act, 1971, a legal action for 'wrongful dismissal' is a common-law action for breach of contract by unjustifiable dismissal. Although it is envisaged that industrial tribunals will one day hear actions for wrongful as well as for unfair dismissal, at present the former are heard in the ordinary civil courts.

To succeed in a claim for wrongful dismissal, the employee must show that he was dismissed without proper notice (or payment in lieu thereof) or, in the case of a fixed-term contract, before the end of the term. He will then be entitled to damages for loss of earnings (including commissions and pension contributions which the employer was under a legal obligation to pay).

If he has lost an opportunity to advance his professional reputation he may receive damages. He cannot, however, get damages for injury to his existing reputation (for instance, if the way he were dismissed would make it harder to find new employment).

In accordance with the usual principles of assessment, damages will be reduced by the extent to which the employee has, or ought to have, reduced his losses by obtaining new employment.

The employee is entitled to compensation for only what he would have received if he had not been wrongfully dismissed. Therefore, he is entitled to receive damages which, after tax, will be equal to his lost earnings, likewise net of tax. As the first £5,000 of damages are free of tax, the damages will be reduced accordingly.

Naturally, it will be a defence for the employer accused of wrongful dismissal to show that the employee's behaviour had given good cause for the dismissal.

An employer has the right to dismiss an employee summarily for incompetence, insubordination, negligence or similar failings. However, it is impossible to state as a general principle how much such failings must be present in order to justify a dismissal. The test is whether the acts or omissions of the servant are so serious as to show his intention no longer to be bound by the contract of employment. Consequently, it is unlikely (but not impossible) that an isolated instance of rudeness or thoughtlessness will justify summary dismissal.

Discrimination

The Race Relations Act, 1968, and the Sex Discriminations Act, 1975, contain detailed provisions to prevent discrimination against employees or potential employees on grounds of race, sex or marital status. Any person who considers that he or she has been so discriminated against should seek legal advice or contact the Race Relations Board or the Equal Opportunities Commission.

13 Financial Law

Banking Law

Cheques

A cheque is any document which is signed by one person and which unconditionally orders his banker to pay on demand a specific sum to, or to the order of, another person or to the bearer of the document. A person who signs the cheque is known as 'the drawer', his bank is 'the drawee', and the person in whose favour the cheque is written is 'the payee'.

Uncrossed Cheques

If a cheque is uncrossed, the drawee bank can pay if the cheque is presented to it by the payee or by anyone in whose favour it has been endorsed. If the cheque is payable 'to bearer', the bank may pay whoever holds it. The payee can present the cheque and receive payment personally. He does not have to pay into his own bank account in order to obtain payment.

Crossed Cheques

If a cheque is crossed, then in practice it can generally be presented to the drawee bank only by the payee's own bank ('the collecting bank'), who will then credit the payee's account. This is because if payment were made directly to whoever presented the cheque for payment and that person turned out not to be the rightful owner, then the bank would have to pay out a second time when the true claimant appeared. Consequently, a bank will not cash a crossed cheque 'over the counter' unless it is absolutely certain that the person presenting it is the payee.

The advantage of a crossed cheque is therefore clear. It will be useless to anyone who dishonestly acquires it unless he can arrange for it to be collected through his or some other person's bank account. Even if he manages to do this, the payment is usually easy to trace. Moreover, if a crossed cheque reaches a payee, the debt which it is meant to discharge will be treated as discharged, provided payment is eventually made on the cheque. This is so even if someone other than the payee actually receives payment.

How Cheques Can Be Crossed

A cheque is said to be 'generally crossed' if two parallel lines are drawn across it, with or without the words 'and company' written between them. If the name of a particular bank is written across the face of a cheque (with or without crossing lines) it is said to be 'specially crossed'. A drawee bank has to pay a specially crossed cheque to the collecting bank whose name appears on it. Otherwise, the payee bank is exposed to the same risks as if it had not paid to another bank at all.

Bills often require that the cheque in settlement of them should, in addition to the usual crossing, bear the words 'account payee' or 'account . . .' (the name of the payee being inserted). In fact this gives little extra protection to the payee. The drawee bank is not concerned with the addition. It discharges its obligation by paying to the collecting bank in the ordinary way. If, however, the collecting bank then credits the account of someone other than the payee (for instance, someone to whom the cheque has been endorsed) it will be liable to the original payee if the person to whom it makes the payment proves not to have been entitled to it.

Sometimes the words 'account payee only' are used. It is doubtful whether the word 'only' has any meaning. If it does, it can only be to make the cheque completely non-transferable.

Cheques are sometimes marked 'not negotiable'. This misleads many people into thinking that they are not transferable. This is wrong. Unless marked to the contrary, a cheque is a 'negotiable instrument'. This means that any person into whose hands it passes can enforce payment, provided he gave value for it in some way or another and had no reason to suppose that there was anything wrong with the cheque or with the title of the person who transferred it to him. For instance, it would not matter if the cheque had been stopped. However, if the cheque is marked 'not negotiable', he cannot be in a better position than the person transferring it to him. Nonetheless, the cheque can still be transferred and, if there is nothing in fact wrong, payment can be enforced. (For technical reasons, an uncrossed cheque drawn in favour of a particular payee which is marked 'not negotiable' is also non-transferable.)

Opening a Crossing

Sometimes the drawer of a cheque which has been issued crossed cancels the crossing and writes 'Pay cash'. He may want to do this if the person to whom he is paying the cheque does not have a bank account of his own through which he could collect a crossed cheque. If he does this, the drawer should write his full name by the alteration (although the bank may in practice accept his initials).

Transferring Cheques

If a cheque is made payable to 'bearer', the drawee bank can simply make payment to whoever presents it. (Naturally, if the cheque is crossed payment must be made through his bank account.) No endorsement is required.

However, if the cheque is in favour of a particular payee, then before payment can be made to anyone else the payee must endorse the cheque by signing it on the back. If he does no more than this, he is said to have endorsed the cheque 'in blank', and it effectively becomes a 'bearer' cheque. He can, however, write 'Pay John Smith'. John Smith can then present the cheque himself or endorse it in his turn. There is no limit to the number of times a cheque can be endorsed (but see also the paragraph below on 'stale cheques').

Anyone who is endorsing a cheque can cross it or add to the existing crossing, either by making it 'special' or adding the words 'Not negotiable'. An endorser cannot, however, remove any crossing. A cheque which is originally a bearer cheque can be endorsed in favour of a particular person.

Dishonoured Cheques

A bank's prime duty to its customer is to honour his cheques, provided that this does not involve exceeding the balance of the customer's current account or the limit of an agreed overdraft. If a customer has accounts at more than one branch of the same bank, the bank is entitled to deduct from the balance of the account on which a cheque is drawn the debit balances on the other accounts and, if necessary, to refuse payment accordingly.

If a customer draws a cheque on an account but cannot meet it, the bank is not bound to honour the cheque even if there is a sufficient overall balance if the customer's accounts at other branches are taken into consideration. Usually the same is true even if a customer has a deposit account at the same branch with enough in it to cover the cheque. However, it is unlikely that the bank would refuse payment in this case. Even if the account is only just insufficient to cover the cheque, the bank is not obliged to pay it nor is there any question of part payment.

If the dishonoured cheque is marked 'Please re-present' this indicates that the bank considers that there is a prospect of its then being honoured. If the cheque is marked simply 'Refer to drawer' there is probably no such prospect.

If the bank mistakenly dishonours a cheque when the customer's account is in funds (or when there is a sufficient overdraft facility), the customer may have a right to sue the bank for damage to his credit. If he is in business, he may be able to recover substantial damages. This may be so even in apparently trivial cases since, for obvious reasons, it may be that the smaller the amount of the dishonoured cheque the greater will be the damage to the customer's credit.

If the cheque was not drawn in connection with a business transaction, it may be difficult in practice to obtain damages. It is necessary to prove actual financial loss. A customer cannot claim compensation for mere embarrassment.

Out-of-Date Cheques

A customer could probably not sue his bank for damage to his credit if the bank refused to honour a cheque because it was out of date. Normally a bank would consider a cheque to be 'stale' if it was not presented for payment within six months or, sometimes, a year. In such a case the person to whom the cheque is payable is still entitled to demand payment from the drawer at any time during the usual six-year 'limitation period' (see also Chapter 1).

The rules about 'stale cheques' are much more stringent in relation to endorsements. First, a cheque ceases to be 'negotiable' if it appears to have been in circulation for an unreasonable time. This means that whoever acquires it by endorsement in such a case will have no better title to it than the person who endorsed it. Quite what constitutes a reasonable time will depend on the facts in each case, but usually it will be anything in excess of ten days. Secondly, no endorser can be sued on a cheque which is dishonoured if it is not presented for payment within a reasonable time of the endorsement. Again, about ten days might be the limit here.

The Banker/Customer Relationship

Apart from the principal duty of safeguarding their customers' money and honouring their cheques, banks often perform other services for their clients. These include:

1 Giving references. It is general practice for a bank to give bankers' references to be taken up through their own banks by persons interested in their customers' creditworthiness. This may be for a private or for business purposes. For instance, a landlord who is asked to approve an assignment of a lease will normally ask the prospective tenant's bankers whether they consider him good for the rent.

Despite this, there is some doubt whether a bank can assume that it has its customer's permission to disclose information in this way, at least where private accounts are concerned. If the information which it gives is inaccurate it may in some circumstances incur legal liability to its own customer if the reference unfairly discredits him, or to the enquirer if he is misled. However, the law on this subject is not clearly settled.

2 A bank is contractually bound to keep secret its knowledge of its customers' affairs. It may break confidence only in exceptional circumstances, such as when it is compelled to do so in the course of legal proceedings.

3 It is common for a bank manager to give his customers investment advice. If this advice can be shown to have been negligent and the customer has suffered loss as a result, the customer might well have a claim against the bank. (Naturally, the mere fact that a recommended investment proves unprofitable is not enough to show negligence. Also, where stock exchange investments are concerned, the bank will probably have taken stockbrokers' advice which would relieve them of liability.)

4 If valuables are deposited with the bank, it will be liable to the customer for loss occurred by its failure to take as much care of them as its security facilities allow. This will still be so even if (as is often the case) no charge is made for this service. However, if the bank accepts valuables only on terms that it is not responsible, it may be under no liability in the event of loss.

Cheque Cards and Credit Cards

A cheque card amounts to a promise by the bank which issues it that it will honour the cheque, irrespective of the state of its customer's account. This promise, however, is conditional upon the terms of use stated on the card being fulfilled. The account of the person drawing the cheque will be debited as soon as it is presented, in the usual way.

A credit card, as its name implies, allows the holder of the card to pay for a purchase without having to repay the bank or company issuing the card until a later date, in accordance with the terms of issue. The person from whom the card holder has made his purchase can obtain payment from the company issuing the card immediately, whether or not the card holder does make the necessary repayment or interest payment.

Mortgages

The Parties to a Mortgage

There is sometimes confusion over what the parties to a mortgage are called. The person who borrows the money and pledges his property as security for the repayment of the debt is 'the Mortgagor'. The person lending the money is 'the Mortgagee'. Therefore, if you buy a house with the help of a building society, you will be the mortgagor and the building society will be the mortgagee.

Usual Terms of a Mortgage

The right of parties under a mortgage will depend upon the particular terms of the mortgage. (There are, however, some general legal restrictions on the rights of a lender. See, for example, Chapter 14.) The following paragraphs are therefore only a general guide to what you may expect to find in your mortgage.

For most practical purposes, if your house is mortgaged in favour of say a building society or insurance company, you will remain in undisturbed possession so long as you maintain the payments due. However, if you fail to do this or if you break some other condition of the mortgage, your mortgagee is likely to have the following rights against you:

1 *Power of Sale.* Your mortgage will probably stipulate a 're-

demption date' on which the money lent becomes theoretically due for repayment. The redemption date is often six months after the date of the mortgage. Under the general law, a mortgagee can exercise his power of sale if, at any time after the redemption date, he serves a notice on the mortgagor demanding repayment of the sum lent and if the mortgagor fails to repay within three months. However, it is likely that your mortgage excludes this power. Again, the general law provides that if at any time after the redemption date there is at least two months' interest in arrears or if there has been a breach of some other term of the mortgage (for instance, one forbidding the granting of a tenancy) then the mortgagee's power of sale arises. Your mortgage will probably contain a provision of this kind.

Although you will have the legal title to the property, this does not prevent the mortgagee from selling. If the mortgagee does sell, the title is automatically transferred to the purchaser. The mortgagee then repays himself out of the proceeds and hands any surplus over to you. Mortgagees are under an obligation to obtain the best possible price. However, this does not extend to having to wait until market conditions are favourable.

2 *Foreclosure.* If you are in breach of the covenants under the mortgage, the mortgagee may apply to the court for an order of foreclosure. If this is granted, the legal title is transferred to the mortgagee who becomes the absolute owner of the property. You lose your right to redeem the mortgage. The court has a discretion to order a sale of the property instead of granting a foreclosure order.

3 *Possession.* Unless there is anything to the contrary in the mortgage, your mortgagee has the right to possession of the mortgaged property even if you have not committed any breach of your obligations. This is because a mortgage is in many ways equated legally with a lease and the mortgagee with a tenant. The mortgagee can enter peacefully without a court order. Failing this, he is entitled to an order for possession from the court. However, your mortgage will probably stipulate that the right to possession will arise only if you fail to observe your part of the bargain.

4 *Suing on a Promise to Repay.* Once the mortgage money is due for repayment, subject to the terms of the mortgage, your mortgagee can sue you on your promise to repay, just as any other creditor can. However, this right is usually of importance only when a sale of the property does not raise enough to pay off the debt in full.

Right to Repay Early

You will have the right to repay the loan before the end of the anticipated term of the mortgage. However, you may have to give, say, six months' notice or to pay six months' interest in lieu of notice.

Less Formal Mortgages

An ordinary house mortgage to, for instance, a building society, will be created by a formal document. The title deeds of your house will also be deposited with the mortgagee. However, it is possible to create mortgages in less formal ways. For example, a debt can be secured by the deposit with the lender of the title deeds to a property, with or without a memorandum recording this. If you wished to raise a second mortgage on your house, you would usually not be able to give the lender the title deeds because they would be with the first mortgagee. You could still mortgage the house by a document alone. The rights which a mortgagee of a less formal mortgage or a second mortgagee may have against you will vary according to the precise legal nature of the mortgage.

Mortgages of Property other than Land

It is not uncommon to grant a mortgage of other kinds of property than land. For instance, a borrower may mortgage stocks and shares or an insurance policy as security. Mortgages of chattels such as furniture are subject to many legal restrictions and are therefore rarely created.

Bankruptcy

If someone's financial affairs reach the stage where he is unable to meet his debts, he may have to face the possibility of becoming a bankrupt. This may happen in one of two ways—his creditors may make the decision for him, or he may take the initiative and declare himself bankrupt.

The 'Act of Bankruptcy'

Before any creditor can begin bankruptcy proceedings, the debtor must have committed what the law calls an 'act of bankruptcy'. Usually the act in question will be non-compliance with a 'bankruptcy notice'. Before this can happen a creditor must obtain a final court judgement for the debt in question. He can then serve a bankruptcy notice on the debtor. Failure to pay or to secure the debt within seven days after receiving the notice would usually constitute an act of bankruptcy.

There are other actions which amount to the act of bankruptcy. These include a debtor notifying a creditor that he has suspended payment of his debts. Also, if a debtor leaves his home with a view to escaping his creditors, this constitutes an act of bankruptcy. So, too, do disposals of property by the debtor which put his assets outside the reach of his creditors or which favour one creditor at the expense of others.

Presenting a Petition

Once an act of bankruptcy has occurred, a creditor may present a bankruptcy petition to the county court (or the High Court if the debtor lives in certain parts of London). The debtor may himself present a petition or file a declaration in court that he is unable to meet his debts, which is itself an act of bankruptcy.

A creditor's petition will set out all relevant details of the debt and the act of bankruptcy. It must be lodged at the court, with a supporting affidavit sworn before a commissioner for oaths. A copy of the petition will then be served on the debtor, in the same way as a writ or summons is served.

There will then be a preliminary hearing of the petition before the court registrar. At this stage, the court will usually issue a receiving order. However, sometimes a court will decide that it would be unjust or pointless to continue further with the bankruptcy proceedings.

The Receiving Order

Once issued the receiving order puts the debtor's property in to the control of the 'official receiver'. Official receivers are appointed by the Department of Trade and are also officers of the court in whose area they serve. Once the official receiver has been appointed, the debtor cannot deal with his property. Any creditors can bring legal proceedings against a debtor only with the permission of the court.

Within a few days of the issue of the receiving order, the debtor must file a statement of affairs giving details of his assets and liabilities. He may also submit proposals for any arrangements which he might make with his creditors. Unless agreement is reached on these, the proceedings will continue with a public examination of the debtor in which every detail of his financial affairs may be discussed.

Adjudication of Bankruptcy

At this stage, the court will pronounce a debtor bankrupt if either the creditors or the debtor himself so requests. When the debtor is adjudged bankrupt he is for most purposes deemed to have been bankrupt since the first act of bankruptcy to have been committed by him up to three months before the date of the petition. The debtor's property is then transferred to whoever is appointed as his trustee in bankruptcy. The trustee is appointed at a meeting of the creditors.

The bankrupt is allowed to keep only clothes, bedding and any tools of his trade. Furthermore, he is entitled to keep for himself out of his earnings after the bankruptcy only what is reasonably necessary for the support of himself and his family. (If he is carrying on a business, he is not allowed to keep any of the profits.)

Distributing the Assets

The basic duty of the trustees is to realise the bankrupt's assets and to distribute as much as possible by way of dividend to the creditors. However, if the assets are insufficient to pay off all the debts in full, not all the creditors are entitled to have the same proportion of their debts repaid.

'Preferred' and 'Deferred' Creditors

Some creditors (known as 'preferred creditors') are entitled to be paid in full before the others receive anything. The most important of such debts are taxes, general rates and the wages (up to certain limits) of the employees of the bankrupt.

The 'deferred creditors' are entitled to nothing until all the others have been paid. These include the husband or wife of the bankrupt (if the debt claimed is in relation to a loan made for business purposes) and, in some circumstances, any partners of the bankrupt.

Creditors to whom the bankrupt has given security for his debt (for instance, the mortgagee of his house) may not have to prove their entitlement in the bankruptcy. If the value of the security covers the debt, they can simply sell the security. If it covers only some of the debt, they can do the same and then prove in the bankruptcy for the balance.

Powers of the Trustee

The trustee has important powers to recover assets with which the bankrupt has parted before the bankruptcy if this was done to deprive the creditors of their rights.

Sometimes a person who is already insolvent but not yet bankrupt pays off one or more of his creditors so that they will not have to prove in his subsequent bankruptcy in competition with the other creditors. If this happens within six months before the presentation of the bankruptcy petition, the trustee may be able to claim the money back. However, the trustee must show that the bankrupt was insolvent at the time of the payment and that the motive for the payment was to give preference to the person paid. If the bankrupt paid only because pressure had been put on him, there will be no fraudulent preference. For example, the bankrupt might have been threatened with legal proceedings.

If the bankrupt has given away property within two years of the bankruptcy (whether to his family or to anyone else) the trustee can set the gift aside and reclaim the property. He can do the same to any gift made up to ten years before the bankruptcy, unless the bankrupt can show that he was solvent at the time. However, if the property in question has passed into the hands of an innocent purchaser, the gift cannot be set aside.

Apart from these specific time-limits, the trustees can reclaim any property which the bankrupt can be shown to have given away with the intention of keeping it safe from his creditors. This is so whenever the transfer of assets took place and whether or not the bankrupt was solvent at the time. In such cases the crucial question of fact is the bankrupt's intention in making the transfer. If he can show it was, for instance, to save tax, it will not be set aside unless it falls within the two-year or ten-year rules.

Discharging a Bankrupt

The court has a discretion to discharge a bankrupt. It will exercise this discretion in the light of the bankrupt's character and conduct both before and after the bankruptcy. If the bankrupt can show that his bankruptcy was brought about by causes outside his control and that he was not guilty of any misconduct, he will be entitled to a 'certificate of misfortune'. He can then obtain an absolute discharge. Often, however, the bankrupt will not be entitled to an absolute discharge. The court may suspend his discharge, perhaps for several years, according to the degree of the bankrupt's misconduct. It can also grant a conditional discharge which allows for property subsequently acquired by the bankrupt to be put towards paying off his creditors.

14 Consumer Law

Recent Consumer Legislation

The 1973 Supply of Goods (Implied Terms) Act gives every consumer a guarantee that what he buys is of fair quality.

Britain's first Director-General of Fair Trading has been appointed to put an end to undesirable trade practices which adversely affect the interests of consumers.

The Consumer Credit Act, 1974, protects those who borrow to buy.

In 1968 we saw the passing of the highly beneficial Trade Descriptions Act. Where a trade description is false or misleading, the trader can now be fined or sent to prison. The court can also order the trader to pay financial compensation to the consumer.

The Misrepresentation Act, 1967, entitles consumers (including house buyers) to claim compensation if they are deceived.

In future, consumer protection is to be further refined, and also developed to produce eventual uniformity with the European Economic Community.

Quality Guarantee

Britain has always had a degree of consumer protection under common law, confirmed and repeated in the Sale of Goods Act, 1893. In every sale the retailer guarantees that the goods offered are of reasonable quality.

In talking of quality, the law refers to 'merchantable' quality, rather than 'fair' or 'reasonable' quality. 'Merchantable' is an old legal term meaning 'saleable', or 'fit for market'. The new Supply of Goods (Implied Terms) Act 1973 defines it thus:

> An article must be fit for the purpose for which articles of that kind are commonly bought, as is reasonable to expect, having regard to

the description applied to it, and the price paid (if this is relevant), and any other factors.

In determining the quality a consumer is entitled to expect, the price paid may be an important consideration. If, for example, an article is bought in a sale at a reduced price, the buyer may be met with the argument that he ought not to expect the same quality as from an article sold at the normal higher price, especially if the sale article was marked with some such description as 'seconds', 'faulty' or 'imperfect'.

A secondhand car must be 'in a *usable condition*, even though not perfect'.

Test of Merchantable Quality

A useful test is to ask whether the average person would have bought the article if he had known its true condition. If not, then the buyer has the right to claim compensation.

Guarantee of Suitability

Besides the guarantee of merchantable quality, the seller also guarantees that the article is reasonably fit for the purpose for which it has been bought. It must be properly designed and it must function satisfactorily. A new hot-water bottle which bursts and underclothes which cause a skin rash are not fit for their purpose and the buyer can claim compensation.

Dealer's Recommendation

Sometimes a customer with a particular requirement in mind may specifically ask the dealer for his advice. If the article suggested does not fulfil that requirement (or fails to come up to the standard and quality a reasonable man would expect of it) the buyer is entitled to be compensated.

Quality Exceptions

There are two situations in which there is no guarantee of reasonable quality implied by law:

Where the seller specifically draws the buyer's attention to a particular defect, eg that a piece of carpet has rough patches, or dye is of uneven colour.

Where the buyer examines, say, an obviously flawed article before taking it. In such cases he cannot afterwards complain of defects which he ought to have noticed when he examined the article.

Examining an Article before Buying

It can be important to establish whether a buyer who was offered an opportunity to examine an article before accepting it in fact did so. Once he decides to examine it, he should make a thorough examination. It is safer, legally, not to inspect an article than to make only a cursory inspection.

The most sensible advice for the buyer of a secondhand car who knows nothing about cars is to rely on the seller's assurance that it is in good condition. If possible he should get this confirmed in writing on his receipt. He will be best advised *not* to look under the bonnet before driving it away. By declining to inspect it he will preserve his rights if it ceases to be usable (or 'merchantable'). His acceptance of the car will then be deemed to be conditional on his later inspection (with or without the help of an expert).

Samples

Where a buyer is shown a small piece of a carpet, for example, and then orders twenty yards of that type, every inch of the carpet when delivered must be of the same standard of quality as the sample. If it contains any defects which were not apparent from the sample piece, the whole roll can be rejected. No legal-sounding phraseology in the order form can be used to deprive the buyer of this right.

Sales by Description

Even if the buyer selects an article himself, he can still complain if it does not correspond to the description on the label. For example, if a raincoat labelled 'rubber-lined' turns out to be lined with some other fabric, the sellers would be liable to replace it.

A buyer who has insufficient knowledge of what he is buying will tend to rely on the seller's description of the article in question. This often happens in the field of antiques, for example, where the dealer's label or description is especially important in matters such as age and period. A misleading description may be an offence under the Trade Descriptions Act, 1968, for which the seller can be fined and also ordered to pay the consumer compensation.

Often the buyer will rely on the description he has seen in an advertisement. If the article when bought is different in some detail from the description advertised, he is entitled to his money back. In one case the buyer saw an advertisement for a 'Herald, convertible, white, 1961'. After buying it he found that the front half of the car was from an earlier model. The seller was liable for this misdescription.

Anyone who has a bad deal after buying in answer to a newspaper or magazine advertisement should write a prompt letter of complaint to the editor. He will be able to bring pressure on the advertiser to offer compensation. If he considers that any of his readers have been treated unfairly, he can enforce sanctions against the firm concerned by blocking future advertisements.

The Supply of Goods (Implied Terms) Act, 1973

Guarantees and Exemption Clauses

From the consumer's point of view the chief defect in the pre-1973 law was that sellers could sidestep the quality guarantee implied by law. All they had to do was to incorporate in their order form a clause which freed them from liability if the articles they supplied proved defective. Often the exclusion clause would be hidden in an elaborate form of guarantee; some even took the form of simulated antique legal documents.

All too often the consumer would find that this pretended guarantee contained an exemption clause which either curtailed or took away entirely his basic legal rights. In particular, it would prevent any claim for compensation if a defect in the article caused injury to the person using it.

In 1973 Parliament prohibited exemption clauses. Where a guarantee is given by the supplier or by the manufacturer it may not detract from the consumer's legal rights mentioned above. It may only add to them. In other words, the supplier cannot now avoid his basic duty to ensure that the goods he sells are free of defects.

Exclusion Clauses in Rental Agreements

The above prohibition of exclusion clauses does not affect purely rental transactions or those for services such as repairs. The consumer must remember that if he hires a car, as no purchase is involved, the rental agreement can still contain exclusion clauses which restrict his rights if the car proves unsatisfactory. Similarly, anyone who rents a television set or office furniture may find the agreement contains exclusion clauses.

Nevertheless, anyone who has been unfairly treated by a rental firm could still complain to the Director-General of Fair Trading. The hirer now has the statutory right to *terminate* his rental agreement after a minimum of eighteen months. If he pays monthly rentals, one month's notice is sufficient.

Agreements for Services

When one sends an article for cleaning or repair, no sale is involved. The agreement with the cleaners or repair shop is for services only, and it is still legitimate for the shop to have printed clauses on the ticket which in effect restrict the consumer's right to a fair deal. Despite pressure to ban unfair restriction clauses altogether, Parliament has not yet seen fit to ban them where no actual sale is involved.

Cash or Credit

Since 1973 the instalment buyer has exactly the same rights to a fair deal as the cash buyer. No amount of legal phraseology in a written agreement will enable a dealer to avoid his basic responsibility to supply goods which are free from defects and fit for the purpose for which they are required. All consumers, whether they buy for cash or on credit, are equally protected unless the circumstances show that the consumer has not relied on the seller's skill or judgement. For example, a dealer in electrical goods may be able to prove that the buyer himself was an expert on hi-fi equipment and bought exactly what he wanted; therefore he could not reasonably be said to have relied on the seller's advice.

In brief, the dealer is responsible if he recommends an article and it does not come up to scratch, or if he misleads the buyer in any way. Since 1973 the seller can no longer escape liability by pleading that he was not a specialist in the goods he sold. Thus, if a pet-shop owner starts selling power-drills or washing-machines he is liable even though he may know nothing about them.

Selling Privately

Only a private individual who does not sell in the course of business is permitted to evade any responsibility for the quality of the article. The buyer must rely on his own judgement. The old legal maxim 'let the buyer beware' (*caveat emptor*) applies. Only if the private seller tells the buyer something untrue or misleading will the buyer have a claim. If the seller simply remains silent, then the buyer will have no claim however disappointing the article turns out unless the seller actually deceives him. For example, false information about the age or mileage of a car could give rise to a claim under the Misrepresentation Act, 1967; however, as a private seller is not selling in the course of business he could not be prosecuted for false statements under the Trade Descriptions Act.

Where the seller is a private individual the buyer can ask him to write on the receipt that the article, say a car, is in 'good working order' or 'with a new gear-box' or whatever the case may be. The buyer should not go ahead in the event of the seller refusing to write down what he has already told him of the article.

Buying at Auction

If a purchase is made at auction, the Supply of Goods (Implied Terms) Act will not protect the buyer. He will generally have no guarantee of quality or of suitability and must rely on his own inspection of the article before the sale. But he can rely on the particular description of the article in the sale catalogue, eg that a carpet is 'Persian' or that a piece of china is 'Wedgwood'. Additionally, he could have a claim under the Misrepresentation Act, 1967, not only if inaccurate information about the article was given in the catalogue, but also if the auctioneer or his assistants gave any wrong assurance by word of mouth.

Consumer Protection under the Misrepresentation Act, 1967

Anyone who is talked into buying an expensive article as a result of unscrupulous sales patter could, if misled, have a claim under the Misrepresentation Act. Before 1967 it was necessary to prove that the salesman was telling a deliberate lie. Now the retailer is liable for anything a salesman says which turns out to be untrue—even if at the time he said it the salesman genuinely thought it was true. In essence, anything said about the construction, origin or performance of an article being sold amounts to a guarantee. If it turns out to be untrue, the buyer can claim his money back.

Proving What Was Said

From the buyer's point of view it is desirable if possible to have the statement recorded in writing, say on the sales invoice. In law writing is not strictly necessary, but it may be difficult to prove what was said unless someone else was present at the time and can remember what the buyer was told.

Fact or Opinion

To give grounds for a legal claim, what was said must amount to a statement of fact and not a mere opinion. For example, describing inferior hi-fi equipment as 'a superb piece of electronics' is a mere puff and not a statement of fact. Again, the seller's claim that a particular brand of soap powder 'washes whitest', or that certain vitamin tablets or medicine will make the consumer feel 'on top of the world', are recognised as part of the language of the advertising business, and too vague to be considered statements of fact.

Careless Statements

Sometimes a salesman misleads a buyer merely because he has not bothered to check his facts, ie he has been negligent. Since 1967 the buyer has a legal claim if misled by the salesman with information which would not have been given if the salesman had bothered to check it. Thus the salesman's 'patter' will usually be legally binding.

The law recognises that it is all too easy to be talked into signing a formal contract as a result of something said by the salesman which is not mentioned in the contract itself. Here the person misled can claim compensation under the Misrepresentation Act even though the salesman's words were spoken in good faith; the seller would be liable unless he could prove that the salesman had good ground for believing it was correct.

Special wording in the written contract excluding a seller's liability for misrepresentations will not generally help the seller to escape liability under the Act. If it comes to a court action, a judge has complete power to make the seller liable, despite any exemption clause.

Auctions

Buying at auction can bring difficulties but here again the Misrepresentation Act may come to the buyer's aid, for example if the sale catalogue gives incorrect information about an article coming up for sale. Similarly, if the auctioneer makes a statement which later proves untrue, the firm is liable.

Most auction particulars state in the printed conditions that the auctioneers are under no liability for the correctness of any statement made about authorship, origin, date, age, attribution, genuineness or provenance of any article put up for sale. However, such a denial will not prevent a judge from awarding damages to a buyer who has been misled by an inaccurate statement, particularly where the seller or the auctioneer ought to have known it was incorrect.

When the Seller Is Silent

Much of the profit of antique dealers comes from the mistaken belief of collectors that they are getting a better bargain than is in fact the case. Where the dealer sees that the buyer is so mistaken, can he legally say nothing and allow the buyer to proceed in his mistaken belief? The rule here is that the dealer must do nothing to induce the buyer's mistake or even to maintain it. By remaining silent he will therefore, in some situations, make his sale without incurring legal liability.

Prompt Return of Goods

Once a buyer discovers he has been misled, or that the item is defective, he should promptly send it back and notify the seller that he is not satisfied. By keeping the article, say a car, after he had become aware that the transmission was defective, and by continuing to use it, he may be taken to have accepted it despite the defect. However, he is not obliged to return the article if he does not wish to: instead he may notify the seller that he proposes to keep it but claim compensation.

The Trade Descriptions Act, 1968

Before 1968 the drawback to all consumer rights to compensation was they could be enforced in a civil court only. Most consumers will fight shy of bringing a court action either because of the expense or because the article's value does not warrant it. Since 1968 Parliament has empowered trading standards officers to bring a criminal prosecution when a consumer has a just complaint. This Act is intended to give blanket consumer protection in two distinct areas.

1 *Goods.* By punishing suppliers who make false statements about their goods.

2 *Services.* By punishing service organisations who mislead customers about the services they offer. The term 'services' covers numerous arrangements, from renting a television set to booking a package holiday.

Although the main aim of the Act is to punish the firms who misdescribe their products or advertise them in an exaggerated or misleading way, the courts now also have the power, besides imposing a fine, to order the firm to pay compensation to the consumer. This Act does not apply to a private individual selling his own property.

Misleading Trade Descriptions

The court can fine or imprison a dealer who incorrectly describes an item and so gives the buyer a false impression of either its quantity, size, composition, performance, manufacture or origin. The incorrectness of the description must be 'noticeable'. For example, the addition of a very small amount of cotton in an article described as 'silk' may not amount to an offence unless the article is 'warranted all silk'.

The misleading statement need not be in writing. It is sufficient if the shop assistant tells the buyer something inaccurate. Similarly, a misleading advertisement would constitute an offence and could entitle a person so misled to compensation. Pretended price reductions which make the buyer believe he is getting an article below the normal price are also an offence.

It is important to remember that any false statement which is to be challenged must have been made *before* the sale occurred.

Misleading Statements about Services

The second part of the Trade Descriptions Act applies to 'services' and is much wider than the part already discussed—which deals only with the supply of goods. The second part of the Act makes it an offence to make misleading statements in connection with any trade or business where (although nothing is sold) services, accommodation or other facilities are provided.

False statements here fall into two categories:

1 Statements which the maker knows to be false (these constitute the more serious offence).

2 Statements which are made recklessly, ie without checking.

The Act does not apply to services rendered by employees. For example, an employee who 'over-sells' himself to a prospective employer and after getting the job proves incompetent would not be committing an offence under the Act.

Applications

The Act has a broad scope: it exists to punish misleading statements by all hire and rental companies, employment bureaux, dry-cleaners, builders, repair firms, garages and a host of other organisations which provide some form of service, as opposed to selling something.

Under the Act the Department of Trade and Industry (in its present form), has the power to define the legal meaning of phrases used in commercial advertising. The effect of this is that customers will in future be able to know precisely what they are getting. For example, a dry-cleaner may advertise a 're-texturing' service for some additional charge. The department, if called upon, can decide exactly what is entailed in 're-texturing', so that a firm using any process that falls short of the official definition would be open to prosecution.

Unsolicited Goods and Services Act, 1971

It was until recently routine practice among some firms to send goods without being asked, no doubt in the hope that the recipient would like the goods and pay for them. This practice is now an offence. Firms can also be fined for sending out letters demanding payment or threatening legal proceedings in respect of goods sent without being ordered.

In fact, the recipient of unsolicited goods may achieve ownership of them without payment by adopting either of two courses.

1 He need do nothing but wait. If the firm sending the article does not trouble to come and collect it, after six months it belongs to the recipient. (The recipient must not do anything to hinder the firm from collecting the article.)

2 Alternatively, when the goods arrive the recipient can write to

the firm concerned telling them he did not order the goods and stating the address at which they may come and collect them. Should the sender take no steps to collect them within thirty days of receiving his letter, the goods sent will belong to the recipient.

Delays

The rule in both commercial and consumer transactions is that, where a time is stipulated, delivery or performance must be made accordingly. Any delay will generally be regarded as a breach for which the customer can claim compensation.

Consumers who place an order, without a delivery date being promised, are still entitled to expect delivery within a reasonable time. A man may order a new car and hear nothing for months: after an inordinate delay the dealer cannot present him with the car and assume he still wants it. Once an order is placed, it is up to the supplier to state when delivery will be made. If this is not prompt enough for his requirements, the customer can cancel his order and look elsewhere. However, by pressing for delivery after a delay has occurred, he will be taken to have accepted the delay.

Claiming Compensation for Delay

A consumer who is prejudiced by unreasonable delay may be entitled to compensation. A contractor who promises to repair a machine or motor car within seven days, but in fact takes three weeks, can involve the customer in expense, particularly if he uses it for his business. He would be justified in deducting from the repair bill the cost of having to hire a substitute machine or vehicle for the two extra weeks.

In certain circumstances the contractor may be under an obligation to compensate the customer for his loss of profits due to the delay. A firm of engineers may undertake to repair or to install a central-heating system in a guest-house in time for the winter season. If they finish the contract three or four weeks late, guests may have to be turned away. The hotel's loss of profit for the period due to their delay would be their responsibility. Normally the engineers would be liable only for an average loss of profits, not for an exceptionally lucrative booking, unless they had been told that a maharajah was coming and that it was essential that the central heating was in working order on that date.

Where no business elcment is involved, the ordinary householder could not expect to receive much compensation, unless the judge thought the inconvenience he had suffered was severe.

Time-limit on Estimates and Offers

Deadlines apply to the customer as well as to the supplier. For example, a housewife may obtain a number of estimates for the installation of a new kitchen. After months of delay she cannot tell a contractor that she accepts his price and expect to hold him to his original figure. Her right to insist on having the work carried out for the sum offered will have lapsed and she will have to negotiate anew.

Again, a man may advertise his old caravan for sale and wish to hold out as long as possible for the highest offer. To speed things up, a prospective buyer is entitled to state that his offer of £500 will remain open only until a certain date; but this does not mean that the buyer is prevented from withdrawing his offer before the deadline arrives and before it has been accepted.

In law, notification that an offer has been withdrawn can come in a roundabout way. For example, a friend may mention to the seller that his prospective buyer has already bought a similar caravan from a local garage. In this case, even though the deadline had not expired, the seller cannot insist on holding the other to his original offer. It is regarded as having been withdrawn, just as if he had told the seller so himself.

Cancellation of Orders

A consumer who changes his mind and decides to cancel his order, say for a new car, is not entitled to do so, save on the ground of excessive delay. In law the dealer can insist on being compensated for loss of the profit which he would have made on the sale. This only applies when the model ordered is in plentiful supply and he has lost the profit on the particular sale, even though he may persuade the manufacturers to accept the car back. He does not have to prove that he has one extra car in his showroom which he cannot sell.

The position is different where the model ordered is in short supply. If there are hosts of eager buyers waiting for it, all a customer has done by cancelling is to shorten the supplier's waiting list. Since he cannot obtain other cars to meet such demand, he has suffered no loss and has no real complaint against the customer for a cancellation.

Doorstep Selling and the Cooling-off Period

The law recognises that the impatience of the consumer is readily exploited, particularly by 'home selling' techniques. Every consumer who signs any instalment agreement at home is allowed a five-day 'cooling-off' period. This right of cancellation without obligation does not apply where the agreement is signed in the showroom or at regular trade premises. Although the consumer has already been handed a copy of the agreement at his home, the company is still obliged to send a second copy by post. After receipt of this second copy the consumer has five clear days in which to decide whether to cancel the transaction. He does not have to give any reason for changing his mind, and is entitled to insist on having his deposit returned before he returns the article.

In the last resort it is the duty of the supplier to collect the article, rather than of the consumer to return it—but the consumer is obliged to look after it properly for twenty-one days.

Receipts and Payments

The right to demand a receipt was given by the Stamp Act, 1891. This made a creditor who refused to give a stamped receipt for any sum over £2 subject to a fine. However, in 1971 the stamp duty on receipts was abolished and with its abolition went our right to demand a receipt.

In practice very few traders would risk losing a purchase by refusal to give a receipt when one is demanded, and most automatic tills print out an itemised bill as a matter of routine. A consumer buying on credit is entitled to a statement of his account showing amounts credited, but a customer paying cash has no legal right to a receipt.

The solution is to pay by cheque. The signature of the payee on the back is evidence that he has received the amount. Since the Cheques Act, 1957, even without his signature on the back a paid cheque returned by your bank can be produced in court as evidence that the payee has received the money.

While a receipt is evidence of payment, it is not absolutely conclusive. For example, where a receipt has been given in error, or where a computerised accounting system has gone haywire and credited sums to the wrong account, a judge would accept an explanation from someone in charge that a mistake had been made and that the account was still outstanding. Similarly, where a receipt has been lost, a court can accept that payment has been made if the person paying is prepared to declare this on oath, or some other witness who knows the facts can confirm it.

How long should receipts or cheques be kept? Most judges take a dim view of creditors who forget about customers' outstanding accounts for two or three years and then suddenly wake up and issue a summons. Few of us keep receipts very long, but in theory we should keep them for six years. After that they are dead, and cannot be sued on. Where the debtor has made part payment, the six-year period starts from the last payment. Similarly, an old debt can be revived by a letter promising to pay, because the six-year period will then run from the date of the letter acknowledging it.

Allocation of a Payment between Several Accounts

Where a customer has a number of accounts with the same firm, he must take care when sending his cheque to state which one he wishes to be credited. For example, he may have three or four hire-purchase accounts with them and they may be threatening to take back his car, which they are entitled to do if he has not paid one-third of the total price. Unless he states explicitly when sending his cheque that it is for the car account (to bring it up to one-third) the company can allocate his payment to any of the other outstanding accounts. Contrary to his intention, the car account could thus remain underpaid, and he would risk losing the car. Where neither he nor the company allocate the cheque to any particular account, the law assumes that it goes towards the longest-standing account.

Consumer Credit and Truth in Lending

The Consumer Credit Act, 1974, gives the consumer who buys on credit a new deal by ensuring that he is informed of the true cost of his borrowing.

For example, a customer sees goods advertised at hire-purchase rates of say 10 per cent per annum. He will be told that for a borrowing of £100 over two years he will pay £20. In fact because he starts making repayments after one month, at the end of the first year he will have repaid half the sum borrowed. Nevertheless, he will still be paying 10 per cent on his original borrowing of £100. He may not realise that he will really be paying a *true rate of interest* of nearly 20 per cent per annum.

The True Rate of Borrowing

All advertisements must now make this clear by stating in the example given that the annual percentage rate of interest is 19·7 per cent. The true rate of interest is almost double the flat rate of interest. It is not permissible for the advertisement to state the flat rate of interest in large print and the true rate of interest in smaller print.

All traders should have a set of tables to assist in informing a customer what the effective rate of interest is for every transaction. If an advertiser offers credit in false or misleading terms he can be fined or sentenced to a maximum of two years' imprisonment.

Consumer Credit Agreements

Every agreement involving credit or any form of financial accommodation up to £5,000 is called a 'regulated agreement' and protected by the various provisions of the Consumer Credit Act. In calculating whether the amount of credit is within the £5,000 limit one ignores interest charges and any deposit. For example, a customer decides to buy a car on hire-purchase at a cash price of £6,000 and trades-in his old car for which he is given an allowance of £1,500 by way of part exchange. He agrees to pay the balance of £4,500 plus interest of £1,000 by monthly instalments. Although his new car costs him a total of £7,000 it is nevertheless a regulated credit agreement since the amount actually borrowed is only £4,500. The Consumer Credit Act covers virtually all forms of credit, but has left unaffected the important distinction between hire-purchase and credit sale.

Hire Purchase	**Credit Sale**
The agreement is lengthy and complicated.	The agreement is usually short and simple.
Basically the article is hired and does not belong to the consumer until the final instalment has been paid.	The article belongs to the consumer from the moment he takes delivery.
The finance house has the right to take back the article if the hirer defaults in payment of instal-	If the buyer wishes, he may resell the article at any time, although if he does so all money

Hire Purchase	**Credit Sale**
ments. It can terminate the agreement by serving notice of default, giving the customer eight clear days to pay the instalments outstanding. Where the hirer has paid less than one-third of the total hire-purchase price, the finance company is entitled to send a representative to take the goods back. Where the hirer has paid more than one-third of the hire-purchase price, the finance company must get a court order before the hirer is obliged to return the goods.	owed under the agreement will have to be repaid immediately (read the agreement to see whether this is the case). If the credit buyer defaults in payment on even one instalment, he then becomes liable to pay the whole of the money owing. The object of this provision is to enable the finance company to sue for the whole balance at once. They do not have to sue for each instalment as it falls due, or wait until the last instalment has become due before taking legal action.
If the hirer is in financial difficulties, the court has power to allow him to keep the goods, provided he pays the new rate of instalments fixed by the court, in the light of his reduced income.	
The hirer has the right at any time to write and insist that the hire-purchase company take the article back. In this case he need not pay more than half of the total hire-purchase price. Provided he has looked after it reasonably well, the court can reduce his payment to less than half. However, if the agreement has already run more than halfway, he will have to pay any additional instalments which fell due before cancellation.	The credit buyer has no right to cancel the agreement, or insist that the finance company takes the goods back, unless they are defective.

Hire Purchase

A hirer who gets into financial difficulties may be better off if all his furniture and belongings are on hire-purchase. If a creditor gets judgement against him the court bailiff will be sent to take his goods and furniture. But the court bailiff cannot take items which are held on hire purchase, because in law they belong to the finance company and not to the hirer.

Although the hirer has no right to sell the article before the agreement is completed, in practice this occasionally happens. A member of the public, who in good faith buys from the hirer a car which still belongs to the finance company, cannot have the car taken away from him. This protection does not apply to dealers, but only to private individuals.

A hire-purchase agreement is so long and complicated that scarcely any consumer ever stops to read it before signing. Nevertheless, once he has signed, he is bound by all the small-print clauses, unless he can claim, under the Consumer Credit Act, that he was deliberately misled. Generally, he will be obliged to keep the article insured against all risks, and to keep it repaired and in good condition.

Credit Sale

The disadvantage of credit sale is that if the buyer gets into financial difficulties, his creditors may enforce a court judgement against him by directing the court bailiff to sell his belongings including those on credit sale.

The credit buyer has the right to sell the article at any time, and to any person he pleases, but if he does so will generally have to pay off the balance outstanding.

The credit buyer is free to treat the article as he wishes and can let it fall into disrepair. He is not obliged to insure it, but would be wise to do so.

Hire Purchase

Where the dealer takes a hire-purchase agreement to the hirer's home for signature, the dealer must send a second copy to the hirer within seven days. The hirer then has a five-day cooling-off period after receipt of the second copy during which he may cancel the agreement without obligation. A hirer who has signed on trade premises is not entitled to change his mind.

Credit Sale

A credit buyer can change his mind where a credit-sale agreement is signed outside regular trade premises. He too is entitled to a five-day cooling-off period during which he may cancel without giving any reason and without obligation, and can get back any deposit.

Harassment of Debtors

This is an offence under the Administration of Justice Act, 1970 punishable by a fine of up to £100 (£400 upon second conviction). Harassment means making unreasonable demands for payment. This may be due to the frequency, or the manner or occasion, of the demand, or of any threat of publicity, which causes the debtor or members of his family to suffer alarm, distress, or humiliation. This includes the use of 'blue frighteners'—notices threatening court proceedings and printed to look like court forms. Similarly, frequent calls at the debtor's home, or threats to send round a debt-collecting van, are unlawful. Any debt-collection agency which threatens to inform the debtor's employer under the guise of obtaining information about him would be liable to police prosecution.

Auction Law

As we have already seen, auctions can pose special problems for the consumer. In particular, he has no legal guarantee of quality under the Supply of Goods (Implied Terms) Act, 1973. Nevertheless, he may be able to bring a claim under the Misrepresentation Act, 1967 (see p 167), or if the circumstances of his case are similar to those outlined below.

Cancellations

If an auction advertised as forthcoming is called off, no one can complain; nor can a complaint be made if the most important items are withdrawn at the last moment.

Buying by an Auctioneer

An auctioneer is not permitted to buy an article for himself without the seller's consent. If he buys without telling the seller the full facts he becomes a trustee of the property for the seller, and he must account for any profit he makes. A seller who thinks he has been cheated may bring a claim against the auctioneer, even after a long lapse of time, unless the auctioneer can prove that the seller consented to the purchase.

An auctioneer who buys an item for himself with the seller's consent cannot deduct his commission from the price.

Auctioneer as Agent

Normally, the auctioneer is acting on behalf of the seller, as his agent. However, the auctioneer does have the power to sign the purchase agreement on behalf of the buyer, once the item has been knocked down to the buyer.

Sales to the Highest Bidder

The auctioneer must sell to the highest bidder unless a reserve has been fixed. A bid is a mere offer and can be retracted by the bidder at any time before the hammer falls.

Reserve Prices

A seller who fears his land or goods may be sold below value is entitled to fix a reserve price, but he must notify those attending the auction that a reserve has been fixed. Prospective buyers are not entitled to know the amount of the reserve price.

If the reserve price is not reached, the person who makes the highest bid cannot insist on buying the item. Once the seller has fixed a reserve price, the auctioneer must not sell below this. If he makes a mistake and sells below the reserve price, the buyer gets the item, but the auctioneer must pay the seller the difference.

Inflating the Price

No seller may take part in the bidding to push up the price unless he has expressly reserved the right to bid himself or to employ a 'puffer' to bid on his behalf (never more than one). The seller's intention to take part in the bidding can be notified in the catalogue. If not, the auctioneer must announce it when the lot is put up. Any buyer not notified that someone would be bidding on behalf of the seller can reject the lot if he has paid an excessive price. Alternatively, he may keep it and claim damages from the seller.

The auctioneer must not pretend to accept bids which have not in fact been made, in order to push up the price. This practice is known as 'taking bids out of the air', and could result in the auctioneer being prosecuted for deception. If two or more persons take part in sham bidding, to induce members of the public to buy at an excessive price, they are guilty of a criminal conspiracy.

House Auctions

When land or property is being sold, the printed conditions must state:

Whether the seller reserves the right to bid.

Whether the sale is 'without reserve' or if there is a reserve price below which the seller refuses to sell.

'The Ring'

One danger, from the seller's point of view, is that dealers may get together and agree not to bid against each other. This will enable one of them to buy a valuable item at a low price, to the detriment of the seller. This type of agreement between dealers is illegal and can involve a penalty of six months' imprisonment (two years at the crown court) plus a fine.

In practice it would be extremely difficult for a seller to prove that the dealers formed a ring against him. However, the seller is entitled to cancel the sale and claim the item back from the member of the ring who bought it. If the item has already been sold, he can claim damages from all the dealers who took part in the ring.

Package Holidays

If a package holiday proves disappointing, this may be because the holidaymaker failed to read the advertising brochure and booking form carefully. These documents constitute his contract with the tour operator, telling the holidaymaker *what to expect.*

It is advisable to check particularly how many nights are spent in the hotel, the time of arrival, and how many hours are spent travelling from airport to hotel; travelling at night may affect the number of nights actually spent at the hotel.

Additional information given by the tour operator to the holidaymaker, for example on the telephone, will bind the tour operator even if it is at variance with the printed booking form.

Exclusion Clauses

Many companies state in the small print of the booking form that they do not accept the holidaymaker's right to compensation if something goes wrong with the holiday. But no special conditions in the brochure will protect the company against liability for misleading the holidaymaker should they promise him a better holiday than he gets. In this case he is entitled to take legal action.

Legal Action for Holidaymakers

The dissatisfied holidaymaker can either bring an action to claim compensation in the county court for breach of the Misrepresentation Act, 1967, or make a complaint to the trading standards officer under the Trade Descriptions Act, 1968.

The latter is the surer alternative since prosecution for misleading information in a brochure can involve the tour promoter in a heavy fine or even a prison sentence. Magistrates' courts now have the power also to order compensation to be paid to holidaymakers who have been duped. In fact fear of prosecution may produce an offer of compensation from the tour operator before any action is taken.

To complain, write to the tour operator (by recorded delivery) with a full list of your complaints and a request for compensation. If no reply is received within ten days, write a further letter saying that you propose to report the matter to the trading standards officer. He can be found at the weights and measures department of your local authority. The trading standards officer will then investigate your complaint and take action.

Although you must complain promptly, normally one year is allowed in which to bring your prosecution. On the other hand, if the misleading statement about your holiday was made orally, eg on the telephone, the prosecution must be brought within six months.

The trading standards officer will normally institute a prosecution if the firm has misled the holidaymaker: for instance if the hotel is inferior, or the room does not have the amenities promised in the brochure, or the promised swimming-pool is still under construction. The absence of any services, eg entertainment facilities, which the brochure promises may also be made the subject of a prosecution, provided it can be proved either that the tour operator knew that the brochure was misleading when he sent it out, or that he was careless, eg took a chance and did not check whether the facilities were in fact available.

Prosecution by the trading standards officer is not always successful, particularly where the complaint relates to the standard of rooms, meals or other facilities. The tour company can generally throw the blame for such complaints on to the hotel. Even so, prosecution does have the advantage of involving the disgruntled holidaymaker in no expense.

Prosecutions under the Trade Descriptions Act must be proved meticulously, as a breach of the Act is a criminal offence. The object of prosecution is to punish the tour company with a fine. An order to pay the consumer compensation is purely ancillary.

Recent civil claims have made tour operators decidedly uneasy; in one case the compensation exceeded the cost of the holiday and recently the Court of Appeal have extended the law by taking into account a holidaymaker's loss of anticipated enjoyment. Some tour operators now stipulate in their conditions of booking that any compensation should be limited to the cost of the holiday, but it is uncertain whether such stipulations really limit their liability.

Cancelling a Holiday Booking

It is possible for a holidaymaker to insure against the risk of cancellation because of illness. But one could be forced to cancel for some other reason. The booking form invariably lays down a sliding scale of charges due on cancellation, which charges increase as the departure date approaches.

One way of reducing such a loss is to sell the tickets privately. One tour operator demanded a fee of 45 per cent on the grounds that records were computerised and hence difficult and expensive to alter. Since the publication of this case many tour operators have been at pains to inform the public that they charge only a nominal transfer fee in such cases. Strictly, the legal position is that they are not entitled to charge any fee at all. In law the benefit of a booking can be passed on to another person unless the conditions of booking prohibit this.

Accordingly, the tour operator should not object to the transfer and ought not to charge a transfer fee.

In the event of a cancellation the tour operator must take reasonable steps to reduce his loss: he must try to sell the holiday to someone else, even at a reduced price. If there is a waiting list for that particular holiday he ought to charge no cancellation fee.

Hotels and Restaurants

Hotel Bookings

Once a person has booked a hotel room for a specific period, and the booking is accepted by the hotel, a legal relationship is created.

If the room is not available on his arrival, the guest can claim damages for general inconvenience. This would include the taxi fare to another hotel, and the difference in price if the second hotel is more expensive.

A guest who does not turn up (even through circumstances beyond his control), must still pay the cost of the room (less a deduction for laundry, cleaning and electricity and food). The hotel need only show that it has done all it could to avoid any loss by re-letting the room. For this reason, a guest should give as much notice of cancellation as possible, to give the hotel an opportunity of accepting another booking for the same date. However, if it is out of season, and the hotel has many vacant rooms, notice of cancellation would not help.

The fact that a guest has not booked is no ground for refusing him accommodation, unless all the bedrooms are in fact full; if so, the guest cannot insist on being put up in the lounge. Otherwise, the hotel is justified in refusing to accept the guest only if he is clearly undesirable, eg dirty or drunk, or appears unable to pay.

Although the hotel is obliged to provide the weary traveller at any hour with food and drink (not alcohol), this may not be easy to enforce in practice. The late-night traveller may have to content himself with sandwiches. Similarly, he cannot insist on food if none is available. The duty of hotels to receive travellers goes back to the time when they were called 'common inns', offering food and accommodation to any traveller willing to pay. A hotel's unjustified refusal to provide either can be punished by a fine. The obligation of a hotel keeper to receive travellers does not apply to boarding-houses or to public houses which specialise in the sale of intoxicating drinks. A public house is not obliged to provide food or accommodation and, moreover, no individual member of the public has any right to insist on being served with drink.

Guests Unable to Pay the Bill

A hotel proprietor can keep a guest's luggage (but not his car) until his bill is paid. But he has no right to detain the guest himself merely because he is questioning the bill or has run out of money. Only when he believes the guest is guilty of fraud can he insist that he waits until the arrival of the police. After six weeks he can take steps to auction the luggage if the bill is still unpaid.

Refusing to Pay in a Restaurant

The danger in refusing to pay in a restaurant to reinforce a complaint is that the proprietor will call the police. This could be very unpleasant and will certainly do your digestion no good.

Complaints against Restaurants

In practice, restaurateurs are more frightened of the criminal law being used against them since the laws about food preparation and hygiene are very stringent. The most effective way of dealing with a bad restaurant is a complaint to the public health inspector of the local authority who will then inspect its kitchens.

When a person orders a meal the law guarantees that it must be of reasonable quality. This imposes a strict liability on the restaurant to ensure that it is fit to eat. If the food makes a customer ill, he can claim without proving the restaurant was negligent.

A guest who becomes ill at a private function or party cannot rely on this strict liability. The guest has to prove that those preparing the food were actually negligent or dirty. This may be a difficult task unless the public health officer is prepared to back the complaint.

Index